The Doctor

Laura Spinney

Methuen

Published by Methuen 2002

1 3 5 7 9 10 8 6 4 2

First published in 2001 by Methuen Publishing Ltd
215 Vauxhall Bridge Road, London SW1V 1EJ

Copyright © 2001 by Laura Spinney

The right of Laura Spinney to be identified as the author
of this work has been asserted by her in accordance with
the Copyright, Designs and Patents Act 1988

Extract from 'Parting' by Emily Dickinson reprinted by
permission of the publishers and the Trustees of
Amherst College from *The Poems of Emily Dickinson,*
Ralph W. Franklin, ed., Cambridge, Mass.' The Belknap
Press of Harvard University Press, Copyright © 1998 by
the president and Fellows of Harvard College.

Methuen Publishing Limited Reg. No. 3543167

A CIP catalogue record for this book
is available from the British Library

ISBN 0 413 75480 4

Designed by Sarah Theodosiou
Printed and bound in Great Britain by
Cox & Wyman Ltd, Reading, Berkshire

To Mikele

My life closed twice before its close;
It yet remains to see
If Immortality unveil
A third event to me.

Emily Dickinson, 'Parting'

PART ONE

Chapter 1

It started as a tingling in the soles of my feet. I felt it as soon as I entered my consulting room: a vibration in the linoleum. The window panes hummed in their frames. I listened, but there was no other sound. And yet it seemed to be getting stronger. I put it down to lorries in the main road, or the hospital incinerator. Then I got on with packing my case, making sure I had everything I needed.

At a quarter past eight I set off on my rounds. The sun reflected off the windows and the railings were warm to the touch. But the street was deserted and the tenements had a vacant, battened-down look about them. The vibration grew stronger and soon it became audible. That's when I realised it must be another march, or a demonstration. Somewhere in the distance a crowd was chanting.

The night before, as I was returning from my rounds, the shopkeepers had been boarding up their windows. A boy sat in the open doorway of a café, polishing a knuckleduster. I didn't give it much thought. For weeks the cafés had been packed with men wearing armbands, smoking and shouting and raising their fists. There's a certain level of violence you take for granted in a city.

At the Salvation Army I turned into an alleyway that was almost sealed off from the sky, the walls were so high. That part of London was a maze of crooked courtyards and alleys. You had to know your way around. I emerged by the synagogue and walked along a street parallel to the main road. By now the chanting was very loud and I could make out the words: they shall not pass. Over and over again, the same slogan. They shall not pass. Whistles were being blown, too. People were shouting orders through a loudhailer, and somebody was banging a drum.

Glancing down the side streets I could see they had been cordoned off at the far end. Mounted police guarded the entrances and beyond them, in the main road itself, was a concentrated mass of people. Each time I reached a cross-section and turned to my right the space beyond the cordon had grown more densely black, until eventually the police line disappeared altogether. I'd never seen such a large crowd, and I didn't like the look of it.

Further on I saw that a lorry had been turned over across the main road. A red flag fluttered from its cab and men and boys were scurrying to and fro with barrels, sheets of corrugated iron and paving stones to bolster the barricade. I stopped to watch them, and after a minute I realised that an old man was standing quietly beside me. He was quite small, and shrivelled, and he leant on a stick. His wrists poking out of his jacket were like thin strips of plywood. Beside him a dog squatted on its haunches. They both gazed down the street towards the lorry.

I smiled and said, 'Good morning,' but he just mumbled and twitched his shoulders. I don't think he knew I was there. He'd stopped simply because something was blocking his path. Suddenly he shook his stick in the direction of the lorry and wrinkled his nose. 'Messy! Messy!' he muttered out loud, 'Sweep it up. In the morning, before she sees. But not me! Oh ho... no you don't...

not me!' He kicked angrily at the air, then turned and scuttled past me, sniggering, with the dog at his heels. I watched him for a few minutes, worried that he would head into the crowd. But he kept walking straight ahead, occasionally shaking his stick.

My first patient was Cyril Rose, who lived on one of those side streets, just a few hundred yards from the main road. His brother Benjamin opened the door. They were identical twins. Cyril was asleep in an armchair with his mouth open. His hair fanned out against the cushion and yellow flakes of skin peeled off his chin and nose. They both had the same white shock of hair, even though they weren't yet fifty.

When Cyril was awake, the two brothers bickered. Cyril lost a foot in the war, while Benjamin survived intact. Later, Benjamin's fiancée ran off because of something Cyril did. Now he was crippled by the pain in his foot, which had been amputated twenty years earlier, and Benjamin suspected him of faking it. Cyril was terrified that Benjamin was trying to poison him, so that he could run off and join his fiancée. The two loathed each other and yet they were bound together.

Benjamin hovered nearby while I took Cyril's pulse and removed a couple of phials from my case. Afterwards he thanked me with a bitter smile. When I first came to London, he refused, on behalf of his brother, to be treated by a woman. I explained, as I always did in such situations, that I was the only doctor in the practice. Ever since then he had been civil, but no more. He let me in, answered my questions, and showed me out. But now, just as I was about to leave, he said wistfully, 'Listen to that.'

He was frowning at the window. There was a net curtain across it, yellow with dirt, so you couldn't see out. I asked him if the noise of the crowd worried him. After all, it was close and his brother was helpless. But he shook his head. If anything, he said, he pitied them. The fight in the street was between two types of people: those who wanted a war with Germany and those who didn't. But they were all wasting their time, because the decision had already been made. It was the politicians who ordered the wars, and the men in the street who gave up their lives for them.

It was then that he asked me if Cyril was going to die. It was the first time he'd mentioned it and I was surprised, because rather than hope or anticipation there was fear in his voice. I couldn't be sure, I said, but judging by the amount of morphine Cyril needed, it wouldn't be long. He thought about this. Then in a quiet voice he said, 'You know, doctor, some people think I hate my brother. But how can I? He's my brother. We've always been together.' I replied, to reassure him, 'Of course, that's natural.' We looked at each other and at that moment I felt a great affection for him. He got to his feet. At the door he said goodbye and shook my hand.

The next few calls took me away from the crowd, though the noise of it followed me, as if I were being pursued. It occurred to me that there might be casualties and I hurried, so as to get back to the surgery in good time. Politics didn't affect me, except when they filled my waiting room. But I was struck by Benjamin's idea, that if you were born in a certain time and place, you couldn't avoid dying. At another time, however, you might live, just because your government had decided there would be peace. It was all down to chance, and the accident of birth.

By lunchtime, when I made my way back, I saw that a riot had broken out. The roar was deafening. Men were running and hurling bricks and there were policemen on foot as well as on horses, brandishing batons. It hadn't spilled out of the cordon, but I knew about crowds; there was no telling what might happen. Beyond the main road the streets were empty, but every now and then a face swam up to a window. Behind their walls, people were waiting. As soon as I turned into my own street I noticed two figures sitting on my doorstep: a man and a boy. The boy was doubled over and my first thought was, I'm too late. It's started.

Coming closer, I saw that the man was Paul Janowitz. Paul lived with his sick mother on the first floor, sandwiched between my flat at the top and the surgery on the ground. Local people said he was connected with the Jewish mafia, but that was just hearsay. All I knew was that he was gentle with the old lady and he didn't like to talk, although he was always polite. The most remarkable thing about him was the way he moved. He hardly made a sound, and all his movements were very precise. Yet he was a tall man. Perhaps it was from having lived with an invalid for so long.

When he saw me, Paul got to his feet and touched his cap. His fingernails were very long, like a woman's. His dark hair curled against his neck and he was smiling, but I could tell he was anxious. The boy's face wasn't visible, because he was hugging his knees. I guessed he was about twelve. Paul said he thought he had broken a rib. He had found him lying in the gutter, just off the main road, when he happened to be wandering past on his lunchbreak.

He hesitated. Then he said, 'My boss'll be wondering where I am.' I told him I would take care of the boy from now on, but first I wanted to know what had happened. I was surprised Paul had been out at all. He wasn't scared of a few blackshirts, he assured me. But his gaze kept straying over my shoulder, in the direction of the main road. The boy had got knocked over and trampled, he explained. He couldn't be sure, but he thought one of the blackshirts, a woman, had rushed the barricade. The crowd had surged forward to block her and that's when the boy had lost his footing. He'd been 'scrabbling round in the dirt' for something.

Between us we helped the boy to the door and then Paul touched his cap again and ran off up the street. My waiting room opens off the hall. I guided the boy through it into the consulting room. He smelt of urine and I guessed he'd wet himself in fear. His fist was clenched and when I prised it open I found it was full of marbles. He closed his fingers tightly and whined, 'They ain't stolen!'

'That's none of my business,' I told him. I just wanted to remove his shirt. But after I'd bandaged his torso and given him something for the pain, I asked him about them. He told me people rolled marbles to bring the horses down. He had been collecting them from under the crowd's feet when this 'stupid cow' ran him down.

I stopped listening after that. I was wondering if a horse's hoof could crush a marble, or at least chip it. If the horse came down the rider might be trapped beneath it. If it slipped it might break its leg. Then it would have to be shot. It made me angry to think of the damage a single marble could do.

The boy was still talking about the woman. He wouldn't be surprised if she had been after his marbles. They were worth something, after all. You could either keep them or you could swap them for cigarettes. I asked him what had happened to her and he grinned. 'She got it worse than me.'

The woman might have been lying somewhere, unconscious, at that very moment. I thought about going out to look for her, but in the end I decided against it. I would just be endangering my own life. So I took the boy home, via a roundabout route to avoid trouble, and when I returned the waiting room was still empty. Usually, in the afternoon, I'd see a handful of patients, but that day the riot kept them away. So I climbed the stairs to my flat. I'd left the window open and the chanting and the drums rose above the rooftops and filled the room. It seemed I couldn't get away from it. I closed the window and fell into an armchair. I wasn't hungry, so I sat staring out of the window at the darkening sky. The muffled rhythm of the chanting must have sent me to sleep.

When I woke it was already four o'clock and the chanting had stopped. By the time I'd finished my evening round the last stragglers had left the main road. Still, though, people remained in their houses. Dusk was falling and now it was silence that boomed through the streets, pressing on my eardrums like a plug of soggy wool. I decided to go back by the main road to inspect the damage. Perhaps because there was nobody about, I noticed how very dirty the pavements were: strewn with litter and smeared with mud and dog mess. The shopfronts, too, were black with soot.

I was wearing the soft-soled sandals I used for work so I meandered to avoid the rubble. At one point I almost lost my balance and looking down I saw that it was a marble I had stepped on. I picked it up and inside the transparent sphere was a bright green twist of glass. I rolled it in the palm of my hand, and held it up to my eye. But there wasn't a scratch on it. I dropped it into my pocket and moved on.

The lorry was still lying on its side and I could see it was leaking oil. A dark pool had collected on the ground inside the rear wheel. When I came closer I saw that it was not oil but dried blood. Someone wearing hobnailed boots had stepped in it and followed a vanishing trail across the cobbles. Whoever had lost that blood was in need of medical attention, and yet I couldn't see anyone. The flag had gone, and on the lorry's tailboard were chalked the words: They shall not pass.

From where I stood I could see down one of the side streets that I had crossed earlier on my way to Cyril Rose's. As I looked a woman turned in at the far end. She was only a speck walking towards me, but I could see it was a woman because she wore a skirt. For a moment I had the impression that I was looking at myself. Perhaps it was because I hadn't eaten, and was feeling light-headed, but I couldn't rid myself of the strange idea that she and I were the only human beings in the world. The streets were utterly deserted, and the emptiness and the blanked-out shop windows somehow made them look wider, as if the crowd had prised them apart.

I started walking again and to distract myself from that

unsettling illusion I thought about Cyril. I once asked him if he could see his foot and he said no, of course not, it's not there. But he could feel its outline and point to the pain. Out of curiosity I asked him to draw it and he did, a swollen golf club with no toes defined. And yet, after the morphine had taken effect, he could no longer draw it. What puzzled me was this: that a real painkiller could work on imaginary pain.

Hearing a shout behind me I turned. The woman had reached the lorry but the distance between us was the same, if not greater, and still I could not make out her face. She was leaning against the cab and one of her arms was raised. Her voice ricocheted off the shopfronts and instinctively I looked behind me, in the direction I had been walking. Perhaps I hoped to see the person she was calling. But there was no other soul around. So I zig-zagged slowly back to her, retracing my steps to avoid the bricks and stones and broken bottles.

When I got close enough it was clear she was in distress. There was a nasty gash on her temple and blood streaked her face, matted her short, dark hair and spattered her blouse. She was slumped against the lorry with her eyes half closed and her skirt hitched up on the radiator. Her stockings were laddered and one knee grazed. She said nothing but I could see she was about to faint. So I took her arm, which was still raised as if she had forgotten to lower it, and wrapped it round my shoulder.

She was shorter than me but heavily built and when I tried to move her, her feet dragged on the ground. It would have been impossible to get her back to the surgery, so I eased her down into a sitting position on the cobbles, with her back against the lorry. She was still conscious and I talked to keep her awake. It was mostly innocuous remarks about the weather, because I didn't want to upset her, but I don't think she heard me anyway.

I opened my case and took out a bottle of alcohol. As I cleaned the cut she seemed to grow more alert. The blood had made the gash appear worse than it was, as blood often does, and she didn't need stitches. But the bruise around it was dark blue and purple and the size of my outstretched palm. Something blunt had hit her hard. I turned away to find a bandage and when I turned back she was watching me. In my surprise I almost dropped the bandage. Until then, I realised, she had been unable to focus her gaze. Her eyes were small and bright, like chips of frozen ink.

'Where am I?' she asked, in a weak voice. I explained that there had been a riot, and she must have been caught in the firing line when a brick was hurled, or a lump of metal. She gave me a dubious look, as if I had brought her there against her will, and then she said, 'What do you mean, riot?' Her accent was Russian or Polish and she slurred her words as if drunk.

She closed her eyes and I was worried she was dozing off. To keep her awake I asked if she had been marching with the blackshirts. She drew her dark eyebrows together and mumbled something about a tablecloth. The only way to get the stain out was to soak it overnight in salt water. It was nonsense but as long as she was talking that was a good sign, and I unravelled the bandage and started to wind it around her head. Suddenly I noticed her bright eyes were open again, and fixed on my face. One eyelid was badly swollen, and there was the shadow of a moustache on her upper lip.

She said, 'Are you a doctor?' and I answered, 'Yes.' She tried to struggle to her feet. At that moment a young woman turned into the main road carrying a basket with a cloth over it. I called to her for help and she stopped and turned towards me. Then, without a word, she turned and walked back the way she had come. I was about to shout after her but by now my patient was on her feet, supporting herself against the lorry. She kept insisting she was 'quite all right'. Then I heard someone say, 'Need a hand, doc?'

A round-faced man was leaning out of a window above the chicken shop, wearing a vest and braces and chewing on a toothpick. He was a former patient of mine, and his name was Klamm. I told him I was glad to see him and he disappeared from the window. By the time he reached the street the woman had taken a few unsteady steps. She didn't want any help, she said. She paused, then walked a bit further. Klamm and I watched, and after a minute he leaned towards me and said, 'You realise who you're dealing with, doc? You won't get anyone round here playing the Good Samaritan with her. Me, I don't mind. I don't get involved in politics.'

The woman called to us. She wanted to know where she could get a taxi. Klamm and I looked at each other and he set off up the street, still chewing on his toothpick. I walked up to her and while we were waiting I asked her where she lived. She looked at me suspiciously, and I explained that I wanted to be sure the blow had done no serious damage. At that she drew herself up and said, 'My name is Anna Petrova and I serve the best caviar in

London. My restaurant is at...' and she mentioned a smart address in another part of the city.

The taxi drew up a few hundred yards away, beyond the debris, and Klamm got out and waved. We walked slowly towards him, Anna Petrova taking tiny pigeon steps. She seemed to be having difficulty negotiating the obstacles in her path. When eventually we reached the cab, she realised she had no money. I found some coins in my pocket and offered them to her. She thanked me, although I noticed she didn't ask for an address to return the loan. To Klamm's great surprise, she pressed one of the coins into his palm and ordered the driver on.

By now, the streetlamps had been lit. In the distance a crowd was gathering at the doors of the Pavilion Theatre. Klamm offered to accompany me home. I don't remember much of what we talked about, except for one thing. It didn't bother him if there was a war, he told me, because he wouldn't be able to fight on account of his digestive passages. He often had to ask his wife to take over the shop because of his digestive passages. But in that way, because of the war, it was a blessing.

I liked Klamm, and I was grateful for his help, but it was a relief to get back to my flat and draw the curtains against the clear night sky. I warmed some soup and ate it with some stale bread I found in the cupboard. As I cleared the plates away, I thought about Anna Petrova. I couldn't help regretting that I would never see her again; partly because of the strange impression she had made on me, and partly because of a more general feeling I had, that she would be an interesting person to know.

My last thought before I went to sleep was that tomorrow was Saturday. Morris was coming over, and I wouldn't have to think about work for two whole days.

Chapter 2

I'd been looking forward to seeing Morris all week. In the morning, when I woke, I lay in bed thinking about what to wear. To save having to change later I chose a green cotton dress with buttons down the front. It gave me an idea for a game.

When I was young I often used to play at being a doctor. Later on, after I became one, I still played games. For instance, if I saw a man in the distance with a twisted limb or acting strangely I had to come up with a diagnosis. It was just a way of passing time. But with Morris, naturally, the games were of a different sort. After breakfast I decided to go for a walk.

Outside the sun was shining and everything was back to normal after the riot. Windows were open in the buildings opposite, and women were leaning out to shout to each other or to the children playing in the street. A man had placed his chair on the cobbles to enjoy the sunshine. He had rolled his shirtsleeves up to the elbow. When he saw me he nodded and smiled.

In the main road it was business as usual, too. The lorry had been shifted and the debris cleared. The people milling about were carrying shopping baskets not paving stones, chatting in little groups on the pavement as if nothing had happened. At the corner, outside Samuel Stores, a little crowd stood huddled around the bookie. His fraying top hat was visible above the sea of heads and he was shouting the odds. I walked a little way along the main road, crossed over and headed down a narrow side street.

The street led me into the shabby square where they hold the bird fair every Saturday. At the entrance a boy with a mynah bird asked my name and repeated it slowly, separating the syllables, until the bird snapped it out. I laughed. Further on the cages were stacked closely together, so high in places that you couldn't see beyond them. There were starlings, doves, budgerigars, all manner of warblers and lapwings. They made a terrible din, shrill and loud, and I began to feel uncomfortable. The sky was open above me but the sound seemed to close in on all sides. I spun round, looking for a gap in the cages, but I couldn't find one. Just then I felt a hand on my elbow. It was the boy with the mynah bird. He guided me out the way I had come, then disappeared inside again. I wanted to thank him, but when I looked back he was gone.

I had a sudden desire to see the river and from there it was only a short walk. I knew a jetty which was quite hard to find, so there was never anybody about. It was completely separate from the docks. To get there you had to wind through alleyways and cross what looked like somebody's backyard, except it wasn't. Then suddenly the river opened up before you. People used to say that part of the city was ugly, but that's because they didn't know my jetty. When I got there a warm breeze was blowing and the sun sparkled on the water. I walked right out to the end and sat down on the rough wooden planks. My heart was still racing and my hands felt clammy. I'd never suffered from claustrophobia before. It was a strange sensation.

Out in the channel a tug was towing a barge upstream. The barge was full of mud and rubble, covered in rust its entire length. It was more like a floating skip than a barge. But at the bow, on a sort of poop deck, a man sat on an upright wooden chair. He wore oilskin trousers and a flat cap, and he was smoking a cigarette with his legs crossed. He turned to look at me, then tilted his head and rotated the hand holding the cigarette in a mock-regal wave. I laughed and watched him glide past. I thought of Morris and made up some rules for our game. Then I closed my eyes and lay back with the sun on my face, listening to the water lap against the jetty.

A whole collection of images began to drift through my mind, and I was happy to let them. There was Paul Janowitz sitting on the bow of a rusty barge, raising his cap to me. Behind him a small boy clambered over the rubble, searching disconsolately for something. For a brief moment Morris's face smiled down at me, eclipsing the sun. Then I stood facing him on the jetty, and the river behind him, and I knew that the game was over. He made a gesture, and I looked over my shoulder. A woman was standing on the riverbank, clasping a furled red flag. As I watched she turned and walked away with tiny pigeon steps. I looked down, and saw that I was completely naked.

It was a dream and yet I wasn't asleep. When I opened my eyes the sun had dropped in the sky. I lay there, thinking about Anna Petrova, wondering what would bring such a woman to that part of the city. Her clothes were well-made and it didn't seem likely that the crowd had swept her there, but she hadn't been frightened. The air began to cool and I remembered that shortly I would be seeing Morris. The thought filled me with pleasure and excitement. I got up and strolled back towards the little square.

My flat consisted of one main room, with a little kitchen curtained off. So the front door opened into my bedroom. When I first arrived I owned no furniture, but since then I had collected the essentials. There was my bed in the corner and a wardrobe whose hinges had rusted long ago, so that I'd had to remove the door with the mirror and prop it against the wall. Then there was the little wooden table with the wireless set, a single armchair and a couple of dusty bookcases with a lamp on top. The window looked out over the backyard to endless rooftops and pigeon coops, factory walls and smokestacks. You could see the black plume rippling out of the hospital incinerator about a mile away. Beyond that the city vanished in a haze.

I brushed out my hair and made up the bed with clean sheets. I put the door on the latch and turned the armchair round to face it. Then I sat down to wait. The next time I looked out of the window, dusk had fallen. I didn't close the curtains or turn on the lamp. But sitting there in that comfortable chair, with darkness falling around me, I was filled with a sense of foreboding. For some reason I was convinced it was Sunday, and I had missed my meeting with Morris. I quickly realised I hadn't, of course. It isn't so easy to lose a day.

In the distance a clock struck eight. I was counting the chimes when I heard footsteps on the stairs. Morris pushed the door open and at the same moment I stood up from my chair. I could just about make out his face. But before he could speak I started to unbutton my dress. I did it very slowly because my fingers were trembling. When the last button was free I slipped it over my shoulders and it fell to the floor.

The game was, to keep a straight face. But there were certain rules. For instance, each garment had to be folded or rolled and placed neatly on the chair. That way it took a long time. For Morris's part, if he spoke, one item of clothing would go back on. If he touched me they all went back on. Of course he didn't know these rules, but that was part of the game.

I removed my shoes, and then I started on my stockings. To begin with, I didn't think I'd pull it off. Morris kept looking at his feet in embarrassment. So I had to pretend he wasn't there. In my mind it was just a normal evening, and I was alone in my flat. Pretending made the little hairs at the back of my neck lift and my heart beat faster. At the same time I had a powerful urge to laugh. I resisted, though, because by now Morris was playing the game too. His eyes flickered up and down my body, and there was a look of concentration on his face.

Finally I had nothing more to remove. Morris didn't move or speak. I think he was pretending too. In his case, he had intruded on a naked stranger who hadn't noticed him. So he couldn't interrupt. If he did, the stranger would scream and he would be arrested. We stood facing each other, and neither of us said a word. Then he came and put his arms around me. We pressed our bodies together and I smiled at him, because the game was over and there were no winners. Or if there were, we'd both won. He kissed me and together we fell onto the bed.

The next morning I was woken by bright sunshine pouring through the window. Morris was still sleeping and I didn't want to disturb him. So I got out of bed and stood beside him, looking down. I liked his crooked nose and the way his blond hair fell across his eyes; his long, slim legs and the white scar on his hip. Ten years earlier, he had bitten off the tip of his tongue in a motorcycle accident. He was roaring down a country lane bordered with lime trees, when the sun flashing through the trees triggered a fit in his brain. He came to me as a patient. Later we became lovers. He spoke with a lisp, but he'd never had another fit.

Wandering round the flat, I came across the marble I had picked up in the main road, and held it up to the light. It was amazing to think that such a beautiful thing could be used as a weapon. Morris was awake by then, so I told him about the boy who had got trampled searching for marbles. He laughed. I told him he could go back to sleep if he wanted. He smiled and said, 'Come here.' I got back into bed and he put his arms around me. Lying there, breathing in the smoky smell of his skin, a sort of languor came over me. I fell asleep and the next time I woke it was noon.

Morris lit a cigarette and propped himself up on his elbow to watch me dress. I leant across to kiss him. He put his arm round my neck and pulled my face down to his. He said we made a 'good couple' and one day he'd like to marry me. I said, 'I'd like that too,' and I sat on the edge of the bed in a shaft of sunlight. But as hard as I tried, I couldn't imagine us as husband and wife. Somehow it wouldn't be the same. For a start, would we still play games? He laid his head in my lap and closed his eyes. The smoke from his cigarette curled up through the sunlight and I stroked his hair. We stayed like that for a long time and I felt very peaceful. Perhaps it wouldn't be so bad to be married to him after all.

Morris sat up and asked me if I'd go dancing with him that evening. I would have like to, very much. But it was Sunday; there was no dancing. When I pointed this out to him he seemed disappointed. He'd remembered that his landlord wanted to see him that afternoon. He wouldn't mind skipping it but he wanted to stay in his good books. I told him it didn't matter. He yawned, and stretched, and lit another cigarette.

After the first lungful he announced he was so hungry he could 'eat a horse'. I fried some sausages and we ate them with mustard and bread. Morris wolfed his down and wiped his plate with the bread. At two o'clock he said he ought to be going. I told him I'd walk with him as far as the main road. I wanted to pick up some groceries. On the way downstairs we heard voices coming from the Janowitzes' flat. The old lady was speaking in a language I didn't understand. It had the quality of all foreign languages you hear spoken: you can't imagine how individual words could be picked out of the stream. But every so often Paul would say 'Yes, mama,' or 'No, mama'.

I stopped by Samuel Stores and watched Morris go a little way. His heels tapped on the pavement and he was whistling a tune. He looked back over his shoulder and waved. At that moment I imagined he was my husband, going off to work. I found it funny, and yet it wasn't an unpleasant idea. Then I turned into the shop and to my surprise, it was full of people.

There was only one reason why people congregated in Samuel's like that, and it wasn't to buy groceries. Sure enough, a ginger-haired man stood resting one elbow on the counter, reading out loud from a newspaper. Samuel himself stood behind the counter, frowning and shaking his long beard. In front of him lay a pile of newspapers. The headline read, 'Policeman Critical After Worst Violence Yet.'

The ginger-haired man was reading about the riot. From what I could gather the blackshirts had planned to march to a certain location where their leader would give a speech calling for peace with Germany. But local people had refused to let them through. Many of them were Jews and Communists. (At this point the man looked up from the newspaper and grinned. A few of the customers laughed; he cleared his throat and continued.)

There were violent scenes, and after a brief consultation with the chief of police, the blackshirt leader had decided to turn back. It was then that scuffles broke out between the locals and the police, and an officer was injured. He had lain unconscious and bleeding for an hour before he was rescued.

(Here the man paused and a woman giggled. Somebody told her to be quiet and he went on, reading out a quote from the police chief.) The chief paid tribute to the injured officer and announced there would be a full investigation into the incident. Then he spoke of his deep shame and regret that, in this day and age, a crowd could stand by and watch instead of helping a man in need. This man had been doing no more than his job, which was to protect the public and keep the peace. Yet he had been viciously attacked and left for dead.

The ginger-haired man stopped reading and folded the newspaper. An old man at the other end of the counter said something in a hoarse whisper. The man beside me told him to speak up but his voice remained a whisper. When he had finished Samuel said, 'What he says is, the son of his wife's brother works as a porter at the hospital. And according to him, the policeman died this morning.' There was a silence, then everybody started talking at once. Samuel shook his beard again and said, 'Bad business, bad business.'

I paid for my groceries and left the shop. The street had that still, timeless feeling of a Sunday afternoon. Walking along, I found myself wondering about the police chief's comment, and in particular the phrase 'in this day and age'. I wondered if people were using it a thousand years ago. Did they behave differently then from now? But I quickly forgot about it, because it was just a manner of speaking. The important thing was that a man had died. I pictured the bloodstain by the lorry. If I'd got there sooner I might have been able to save him. It was an idea I often had, that I could have done more. But of course you can't help everyone.

When I got home I climbed the stairs and paused outside the Janowitzes' flat. But there were no voices and the house was quiet. Upstairs I switched on the wireless and turned the dial to find some music. I read for a couple of hours and then, because I had nothing better to do, I went to bed early. Some time during the night I dreamt that Cyril Rose spoke to me. I couldn't hear what he was saying but I knew he was angry. The words exploded from his lips in little gusts and the red rim of his eye flickered. He pointed to his foot and I saw that where once there had been nothing there was now a raw red stump. It had no toes and resembled more a fist turned inside out than a foot. I knew I was dreaming, and yet I pitied him.

Chapter 3

All through Monday that dream stayed vivid in my mind. It coloured my waking thoughts and I couldn't shake it. For the rest of the day, everything took on a strange, unreal quality.

First there was the story about the babies. It was on the wireless, or perhaps I read it in the newspaper. Two women had shared a room in a maternity hospital and when the nurse brought the first baby in and offered it to one of them, she said it wasn't hers. So the other woman took it. Later she became convinced she had the wrong one. It was because the fingernails weren't properly formed, even though her baby had been full term. But by then it was too late and she brought the little girl up as her own. The women remained friends and years later admitted to each other that there had been a mistake. When they came to tell their daughters, the girls announced that they had known for years.

That story stuck in my mind and I couldn't stop thinking about it. It was the idea that a few words uttered at a certain moment could change the course of four people's lives. And yet, in many ways, it made no difference. The girls were just as happy, or unhappy.

In the afternoon I took surgery as usual. Among the patients waiting to see me was Benjamin Rose. Five people had arrived before him, so he had to wait his turn. He sat in the corner by the door, very upright, fingering the rim of his felt hat. Each time I showed a patient out and called the next one in, he looked down at the hat. White tufts of hair stood out at right angles from his head.

When it came to him, I sat down behind my desk and he took the chair opposite. I realised he was upset. His lower lip was trembling and he stuttered a bit. I told him to take his time and I think he was grateful. He took a deep breath and announced that he wanted to talk to me about Cyril. But first he wanted to get something straight. 'What I told you, about him and me, the way it is, you remember?' I nodded. He stopped to pass the back of his hand across his mouth and clear his throat.

Then he spoke very rapidly: 'This morning, we went to the shops. He was in his chair as usual. I left him outside the greengrocer's and went in for some parsley. They keep it on the counter. When I came out, I heard him say "Ben". But he wasn't talking to me. He was talking to the greengrocer. At first I thought he was fooling. But when I tapped him on the shoulder, he looked me straight in the eye and said, "Who are you?" It was no joke. He didn't know me. His own brother.'

There was a pause, and then he repeated the last thing he'd said: 'His own brother, and he didn't know me.' I explained that it was probably just a temporary lapse. Sometimes the drugs had that effect. But Benjamin shook his head in an agitated manner and said, 'No, no.' According to him, the drugs were rotting Cyril's brain. It had got to the stage where he was either asleep or in pain. When he was asleep, he had terrible dreams. He'd start screaming and Benjamin wouldn't be able to wake him.

He was losing his mind. Not only that. Sometimes he wet his bed, or worse.

He broke off suddenly and sat fiddling with the rim of his hat, twisting it back and forth in his bony fingers. He swallowed a couple of times and blinked. But a tear escaped and he wiped it quickly away. I looked away. After a pause I told him there was nothing more I could do for Cyril. In a voice choked with tears, he said, 'Excuse me, doctor, but that's not true.' I didn't reply, and he got angry. He said: 'There's dignity in death. But this, it isn't dignified.'

A chair scraped in the waiting room outside and a woman coughed. But Benjamin didn't take his eyes off me. It was clear he had thought the whole thing out. To play for time, I got up and walked round the desk. If I understood him right, he was asking me to break the law. But then the law isn't always dignified.

I put my hand on his shoulder and said, 'I am a doctor. My job is to cure people, or at least ease their pain.' But he misunderstood me. He said, 'Yes, yes,' and his eyes shone, as if I had promised to help him. We looked at each other, and I shook my head.

Benjamin bent his head over his hat. His shoulders dropped and he sighed. A moment later he got to his feet. He stood looking down at me with that familiar bitter smile and said, 'That's all right, doctor. Thank you all the same.' Then he stuffed his hat on his head and left. I heard his footsteps slowly cross the hall and the front door slam behind him.

I sat down in my chair and stared into the waiting room. Everything he had said was true, and I wasn't sure I had made the right decision. There wasn't any time to think about it though, because just then a figure appeared in the doorway. It was Anna Petrova. She had been sitting with her back against the partition wall to the right of the door. She wore a brightly coloured scarf folded around her forehead. It was tied at the back, in the gypsy way, with a knot at the base of her skull. I hadn't expected to see her again. But now she was here, standing in my consulting room, I felt a shock of pleasure.

She sat down in the chair that Benjamin had vacated and asked casually, 'Are you going to help him?'

I was taken aback. 'Don't you realise what goes on between a doctor and a patient is confidential?' I asked.

'I can't help it if your walls are too thin.' she replied, indignantly. She looked hurt and I immediately regretted my outburst, even though I was in the right. To change the subject I asked her how she was feeling. The grey light from the window, which looks out onto the backyard, fell across her face, and I could see that the bruise had settled into the socket of her eye. She lifted the scarf to show me the wound. Then, as if to explain, she said: 'I don't like my clients to see me like this. It puts them off their food.'

I asked her about headaches but she said no, she'd had none. So I asked her if she could remember what had happened to her. She hesitated before answering, 'Yes.' There was a pause and I suggested it might help her to tell me. She frowned. But after a minute, and in a rather rambling way, she started to tell the story.

She had been marching with the blackshirts, even though she wasn't a blackshirt herself. She was one of a crowd of supporters cheering and urging them on from the rear. When the column wheeled into the main road, she was too far back to see the barricade but she could hear the chanting. Then, without warning, the march came to a standstill. 'Nobody told us what was happening. People were turning round in circles, asking, "What's going on?" One man said the road must be up. Another said the reds had run off with their tails between their legs. But all the time I could hear the chanting and I knew it wasn't true.'

After what seemed like a long time the order came to turn round. Without knowing how, she found herself at the head of the retreating procession. Minutes earlier people had been singing at the tops of their voices, waving banners and flags, but now the flags hung at their sides and all you could hear above the shuffling feet were jeers and laughter from the barricade. 'There was this woman, she couldn't keep her teeth from chattering. She was in shock. Everyone was thinking the same thing, but nobody dared say it. The Leader had lost his nerve. Right at the crucial moment, he'd lost his nerve.'

After that things had become a bit of a blur for her. She remembered the jeering and how she couldn't bear it any longer. She remembered breaking rank and running as fast as she could in the direction of the chanting. People put out hands to try and stop her but she swerved to avoid them. She kept running, even though she had no idea what she was going to do. Then the barricade came into sight and a sort of fog came down over her brain. There were a lot of blue uniforms about but they had their backs to her, trying to contain the crowd or persuade the protesters to come down. She singled out one figure on the lorry, a tall, dark young man. He had this terrible sickly smile on his face and he just stood there, perfectly still, watching her. His smile was the last thing she remembered. The crowd closed in on her, and she was still about a hundred yards away when something hard thudded against her head, and she blacked out. She didn't know how she came to be in the side street where she first saw me, but she supposed she must have wandered there in a daze.

She stopped to adjust her headscarf and remove a cigarette from her bag. I explained there was no smoking in my surgery and she put it back again. She asked me what I thought of her story. Politics didn't concern me, I explained, but I found it interesting. She gave me an odd look and said, 'You think I'm crazy.' It was more of a question than a statement. I answered, carefully, that I could understand why she had felt let down. Then she announced that she didn't regret what she had done. If you spent your life waiting for other people to take the initiative you were bound to be disappointed. She asked me if I hadn't found that and I said that, by and large, it was probably true.

She smiled and, taking out a black leather purse, she pushed some coins onto the desk. My first thought was that it was some kind of reward. She had been testing me and I had answered correctly. But of course that was ridiculous. Gradually I realised it was the money I had lent her for the taxi. She said, 'I could have given it to you last Saturday. I followed you from the main road. You went into the bird market and I was waiting for you to come out. But you must have doubled back, or found another way out. Anyhow, I lost you.'

I looked at her in surprise. The tone of her voice was reproachful and yet she had just admitted to spying on me. On the other hand, I could hardly object. She was entitled to be in a public place. I asked her why she hadn't given me the money immediately, in the main road. She shrugged her shoulders. 'I wanted to see where you'd go. You seemed to know your way around.' I asked her if she often followed people and she thought about it. 'No,' she said, 'Not often.' Her expression was quite serious. One more thing puzzled me: if she had lost me, how had she found out where I lived? She grinned and said, 'I asked the man in the chicken shop. At first he wouldn't tell me. So I had to bribe him.'

I didn't know what to say to that, and we looked at each other in silence. Then she announced that she had to get back to the restaurant. I had the impression she was bored of the conversation, but in hindsight I think I was wrong. I showed her out and on the doorstep she invited me to have lunch with her the following Sunday. I was about to accept when she asked, 'Do you like caviar?' I had never tasted it, I told her, but I liked fish. She snorted and said it was nothing like fish. Caviar had a taste all its own and if you hadn't tasted it you hadn't lived.

As a sort of afterthought, she looked up at me with her bright black eyes and said, 'You know, it's really your duty to help that old man.' I didn't reply, because by now I'd realised there was no point. It was just a way she had, of interfering in your affairs and at the same time disarming you. You never knew what she was going to say next, and sometimes it was exactly what you were thinking yourself. So I just smiled and said I was looking forward to Sunday.

We shook hands warmly and she said goodbye.

As soon as she had gone I went upstairs. I'd left the window open in my flat and voices were drifting up from the yard. Looking down I saw Mrs Janowitz and her son Paul. He was carrying her in his arms, about to lay her down on a battered old sofa in the corner. She was talking in that foreign language, only this time he was not responding. When he disappeared inside she fell silent. But as soon as he reappeared with a bundle and a furled umbrella, she started up again. From the tone of her voice I guessed she was telling him off.

Pulling a scarf out of the bundle, he gently lifted her head and passed it underneath, knotting it in his methodical way. He covered her in a faded pink eiderdown, and, opening the umbrella, propped it against the arm of the sofa. I could no longer see her face, but he stood over her, his hands folded in front of him, listening and occasionally nodding. It was a comical sight: a grown man being nagged by an umbrella. After a few minutes he said something I couldn't understand and left the yard.

The umbrella was still for a while, then it started to rock from side to side. Finally it collapsed, and instead of a grey-haired old woman a glossy brunette emerged. That meant it was Mrs Janowitz's day for receiving visitors, so I let myself out of the flat and went downstairs. As soon as I stepped into the yard her face split into a smile and she opened her arms wide. She insisted that I make myself comfortable on the edge of the sofa.

I always enjoyed talking to Mrs Janowitz. Her legs were ulcerated with arthritis and yet she never complained. I asked her if she would like me to take a look at them but she said no. They were healing nicely, and besides, she had more important things on her mind. I asked her what the trouble was and she told me that on the day of the riot Paul had stayed out until evening. She had been worried sick, but when he came back he told her that his boss had sent him to another part of town on business. 'He is a good boy,' she said, 'but he doesn't always think.' Something was distracting him and she thought she knew what it was: gambling or a woman. It had to be one or the other. Both were serious, but she wouldn't mind so much about debts.

Just then a woman called from the next door yard and Mrs Janowitz answered in her quavering voice. Soon the neighbour's ruddy face appeared above the wall. She said, 'Good afternoon,' but then there was an awkward silence. I got to my feet, because I remembered that she spoke no English. Mrs Janowitz grasped my hand and thanked me for coming.

Upstairs I pulled the window sash down to an inch from the ledge and sat down in my armchair. I was thinking about Paul Janowitz, wondering why he had lied to his mother. Perhaps she had made a mistake. It was none of my business anyway, so I picked up a medical journal and started to read. But the old women's voices had a soporific effect. I very soon fell into a deep sleep, and had the same dream about Cyril Rose I had had the night before. When I woke, it was as if I had dreamed the day in between.

Chapter 4

Morris came over as usual on Saturday. He'd won two tickets for that night's boxing match in a bet. He wanted me to go with him and he was very excited. I wasn't sure. I couldn't understand the attraction in watching two men beat each other until they bled. But Morris said there was more to it than that, and in fact it was a form of art. I was still dubious, but as he pointed out, I'd never been to a boxing match before, so I couldn't judge.

The fight was to be held in a dilapidated warehouse near the docks. It was a warm evening and we decided to walk. Morris put his arm through mine and we soon got caught up in a crowd. The whole neighbourhood seemed to be going to the fight. There was a low murmur of excitement and I was reminded of the evening before the riot, when all the cafés were full and I saw the boy polishing his knuckleduster. The mood was the same, but this time I was a part of it and I felt the excitement too.

In front of us, walking in the same direction, was a group of local lads. At one point two of them leapt off the pavement and started sham boxing in the middle of the street. They danced around in circles, taking swipes but never making contact, until finally they fell on top of one another, each trying to wrestle the other to the ground. The rest of the little group stood round egging them on, and Morris stopped to join them. I laughed and several passers-by turned to watch and smile.

As soon as we arrived at the hall I knew it wasn't a place I'd like to be. The ring had been set up on a raised platform in the middle, and rows of wooden benches filled the space on two sides. The rest was standing room only, and it was packed. The hall was hot and there was a smell of sawdust mingled with sweat. It reminded me of a circus, and in a way, it was. Morris had ringside seats, but the space between the bench and the ring was already full of people swarming up against the ropes. Girls wearing low-cut tops wandered up and down, carrying trays of peanuts and cigarettes. The empty shells crunched underfoot.

Looking round the hall I caught sight of Klamm. He was in his shirtsleeves, and his hair was slicked back and glistening. He was holding onto one of the ropes of the ring, and chatting to a man inside who had a towel round his neck. The man laughed and slapped him on the shoulder in a familiar way. I waved but he didn't see me, and a minute later an excited cheer went up. Klamm stepped back and behind him the crowd parted to make way for the two boxers.

When they climbed into the ring Morris pointed out the one we should be cheering for. He wore red shorts, while the other wore blue. According to Morris he was known as The Kid. He looked very young and nervous, but Morris said he was 'ruthless' when he got going. Besides, he was the local boy and we had to support him. The man with the towel round his neck took it off and threw it to someone on the benches. He made a little speech and I realised he was the referee.

A bell rang. At first The Kid hardly struck any blows.

The other man would lash out, and The Kid would dance backwards and forwards, first to one side and then the other, avoiding his punches. But when his opponent swung a particularly violent punch, throwing himself off balance, The Kid would step in and insert a neat fist into the side of his head, sending him reeling back against the ropes. At those times I understood what Morris meant by ruthless. Each time it happened the spectators would cheer and Morris would clap his hands. Once he turned to me and said, 'He's a genius.' I thought that was a strange word to use, and I didn't reply. I had already made up my mind to leave after the first round.

After the first round I decided to stay for one more. No blood had been spilt but The Kid's opponent looked a little unsteady on his feet. I was curious to see how long he could stand this battering. By the fifth I couldn't take my eyes off them. That's when it occurred to me that the skill wasn't in ending the fight, but in prolonging it. In that way, Morris was right: it was a form of art. Or a game, with rules. Of course there was a certain amount of luck involved too, but that's how I understood it and from then on I began to enjoy myself.

There were a couple more rounds but I don't remember much about them, except that everything that happened seemed to please the crowd. The referee declared The Kid champion and held his arm up in the air. Then the champion removed his gloves and helped his opponent up off the floor. The other man's face was swollen and his lip was bleeding. Supporting him with one arm The Kid waved the other in the air. There was a great roar, the crowd surged towards the ring, and at that moment I realised that everyone in the place was united by one feeling: love for this man. It was a physical feeling and I felt it too. Men threw their hats in the air and tried to climb through the ropes to touch him. When I turned towards Morris he had gone, and the next time I saw him he was in the ring, hugging Klamm and smiling in delight. The Kid had disappeared from sight.

It wasn't until I got out into the street that I realised my heart was beating with the exhilaration of it. After the heat of the hall it was good to feel the cool night air on my face. Morris caught up with me and put his arm round my waist. He was out of breath and his eyes glittered. He pressed his mouth to mine and I kissed him back. The noise of the crowd was still reverberating in my ears and my head was spinning, as if I'd had too much to drink. I told Morris and he laughed. At that moment I wanted him and I think he understood. He tightened his arm round my waist and we walked a little faster.

We woke early the next morning and had breakfast together. Morris told me there was definitely going to be a war with Germany and sooner or later they'd be needing men. He said, 'I've been thinking about joining up.' We looked at each other in silence. Of course it was impossible to avoid hearing about war. The newspapers were full of the latest German invasion and every time you turned on the wireless men were discussing it. But somehow it seemed very distant. People went about their daily lives and it was difficult to imagine things changing. I said so to Morris and he agreed. He liked his job and he'd be sorry to give it up. But he knew his duty too. I could see he'd thought about it, but that didn't make me feel any better.

To cheer me up he suggested we go to a pub near the docks. I couldn't, I told him, because I had agreed to visit a former patient of mine. He didn't seem curious to know who and I was glad not to have to explain. After he'd left I changed my shoes, put on scent and a little rouge, and walked to the bus stop. Two girls of about eighteen were already standing there, giggling and shoving each other from side to side. They both had on American sailor hats and the same bright shade of lipstick.

I leant against the wall, watching a scene unfold on the other side of the road. At the corner a man had climbed up on an old soap box. He was lecturing the passers-by, wagging his finger at them and turning slightly to follow each one past. Each one in turn increased their speed to pass him. But eventually a young woman stopped, and he began to address his comments to her, shaking his head and wagging his finger in an agitated manner.

She kept looking over her shoulder in an embarrassed way, and once I caught her eye. But she stayed to listen. I couldn't hear what the speaker was saying but I did catch one phrase: 'equality for women'. I was surprised, because from his manner I had assumed he was talking on a religious theme. But then I realised that although he was wearing a black shirt under his jacket, there was no dog collar. I had just assumed he was a priest. After a while another couple of people stopped and slowly a little crowd built up. Now that she had company, the woman no longer glanced behind her. She stood very still, gazing up at him. The speaker raised his voice and now he was talking about rights for the poor.

Soon the bus came. I sat on the top deck so that I could

have a view of the river. I walked the last bit, following Anna's directions. But before I found the restaurant I heard someone shout my name. I looked round and there she was, leaning against a column at one side of the entrance and smoking a cigarette. She was wearing a white apron and the same brightly coloured headscarf. Above her loomed her own name in gold letters: 'Anna's'.

The restaurant was small and panelled in oak. The walls were covered in religious icons and faded portraits of figures in uniform. There were no other customers and Anna told me the restaurant was officially closed. She didn't say anything after that. She showed me to a little table covered with a white cloth, and lit a candle in the middle of it. She looked very solemn and I had an idea that I was taking part in some kind of ceremony. She disappeared into the kitchen and came back with a tray. On it was a bottle of vodka wrapped in a white cloth, two small glasses, a dish of green lettuce leaves and another of shiny black stuff.

Anna arranged the objects on the table, removed her apron and showed me how to drink the vodka in the Russian way: in one mouthful, like medicine. All this without speaking. The vodka burned the back of my throat and made my head sing. I must have grimaced because she laughed and refilled my glass. Then she spooned some of the caviar onto a lettuce leaf and handed it to me. I liked the salty taste of it, and the burning ice of the vodka afterwards. I told her it was good and she nodded.

After the caviar came the main course: lamb in raisin sauce. Anna said it was a traditional Russian dish. By now the vodka was warming my blood and I no longer felt self-conscious. I told her I was glad she had come back to the surgery that day. She smiled and I asked her what it was like to run a restaurant. In many ways, she said, it was just like any other business. There were good times but a lot of the work was monotonous. To make the time pass she would get tight in the morning and sip vodka throughout the day to keep herself 'topped up'. That way she never had a headache, but the work became bearable.

I didn't have to encourage her after that. She seemed happy to talk. The restaurant was named for her mother, she said, not her. She'd only really been running it for a year, since her father died. He'd bought it when he first came over from Russia. He had been high up in the military but the communists made it impossible for him to stay. She was only a little girl at the time, so she considered England her home. But it had broken her mother's heart to leave Russia. She died within a year, and after that her father lost interest in the restaurant. 'He kept it going, but not to make money. Only to entertain his friends.'

She asked me if I would like some coffee. I wanted to hear more but I said, 'Yes', because I had drunk too much vodka. She went into the kitchen and when she came back she carried on talking. She didn't think she'd like to go back to Russia. To a certain extent she was curious, but all her memories of it were bad. There was one particular incident that she would never forget as long as she lived. She paused, and a distant look came into her eye, as if she was seeing it all again. She lit a cigarette and told me the story.

A gang broke into her father's house and forced all three of them down into the cellar. They tied her father's wrists and beat him. Then they made him watch while they beat her mother and ripped her clothes and did some other things too. Anna was bundled in a corner and watched the whole thing from there. 'All the way through he whimpered like a puppy,' she said. She asked me if I could imagine what that would be like, to hear your own father 'whimper like a puppy', and I said, 'No'.

I wanted to say something to comfort her but I couldn't find the words. We sat in silence and then she asked me if I understood why she hated the communists. If I had seen what she'd seen, I said, I would probably hold a grudge against them too. People assumed children had short memories, but as a doctor I knew that was wrong. She wanted to know if I felt the same way and I answered truthfully, 'No,' because I had no reason to hate them. Her face split into a tight smile and in an odd way her lips rippled over her teeth. She said, 'You never heard your father whimper like a puppy.'

After that she asked me if I believed in omens. In my opinion, I told her, coincidence could explain most things. She didn't want me to think she was superstitious. 'But when I saw that man on the lorry, I knew it was a sign.' He was the image of the man who had ripped her mother's dress: tall and thin, with a long face, dark, doleful eyes and the same sickly smile. 'Seeing him, it was as if I was a little girl again, back in that cellar.'

He had been sent to her as a warning that history was about to repeat itself. That's how she had come to understand it. And the more she thought about it, the more it made sense. You couldn't deny that there was a lot of similarity between the two situations. Then and now, the communists wanted revolution. They'd succeeded in Russia because the world was distracted by the Great War. Now they wanted another war so that they could take over this country. They were cowards and murderers and somebody had to stop them. 'But nobody will because nobody knows what they're plotting. Except me.'

She stubbed out her cigarette with a trembling hand. Now I could understand why she had attacked the barricade. It was an obsession she had had since childhood. I felt sorry for her and I placed my hand over hers. Neither of us spoke, but when she had composed herself she announced that she had come up with a plan. Before she told me it she wanted to know if I would help her.

I'd like to help her, I said, but I couldn't agree to something without knowing what it was. She looked at me and then she said, 'All right.' It was very simple. She was going to have some stickers printed with the slogan 'War Destroys Workers'. Then she was going to post them all over my neighbourhood. I asked her why there, and she said for the same reason that the communists held their meetings there: because the people were poor, and therefore angry. The only problem was that her plan would have to be carried out at night and that's why she needed me, to act as her guide. 'You know your way around,' she said.

My first thought was that it was absurd. Anyway she would be wasting her time. Nobody would take any notice of her stickers. But I didn't say anything straight away because I didn't want to offend her. She offered me a cigarette and I accepted, even though I'm not a smoker, because it seemed rude not to – it was all part of the ritual. It was the strong Russian type and it sent the blood rushing to my head. The vodka was already pounding at my temples, and all of a sudden I saw myself as if from a distance. It was Sunday afternoon, and I was sitting in a restaurant with a strange Russian woman, drinking vodka and smoking exotic tobacco. I couldn't remember why I was there and then a thought occurred to me. It was more a feeling I had about Anna, that she had come from a place far away, and was headed somewhere distant too. The effect was to make me stationary while she whirled past. I would only know her briefly and yet she would change things for me. That was how I felt and yet I couldn't explain it.

When the sensation passed I realised that she had asked me a question. I said 'Pardon?' She gave me an odd look and said, 'War destroys workers. That's true, isn't it?' She'd thought that as a doctor I would understand. After all, I saw the effects of it every day. I thought about Morris, and Cyril Rose. But before I could say anything she informed me that she was going ahead with it anyway. Whether I helped her or not, the stickers would get posted. She asked me a second time if I would help her. If I said no, she added, we'd never meet again. I thought about it. She was offering me an adventure, something different from the usual pattern. Perhaps because I'd had a lot to drink, the prospect filled me with a kind of excitement. Besides, there seemed no reason not to. It was a free country, nobody would be forced to read the stickers. And I liked her. So on an impulse I smiled and said, 'Yes'.

We discussed the plan a bit more and then, because my

head was beginning to ache, I suggested we go for a walk. Anna agreed and we set off towards the park. I noticed that she walked very fast, forcing other pedestrians to step aside. On the way she put her arm through mine and told me she was glad, because I understood things and now we were friends. She seemed very cheerful and I thought I'd done the right thing, even though her theories were wild.

It was a sunny afternoon and the park was full of people. We sat down on a bench looking out over a large pond surrounded by weeping willows. It was a peaceful place and I felt content in her company. At the water's edge some children were baiting a pair of swans with a long, pointed stick, the kind that park keepers use to pick up rubbish. The swans were hissing and arching their necks, but the children kept on poking at them and laughing.

We watched them and after a while Anna asked me if I was married. I told her I wasn't and in a knowing way she said, 'I didn't think so.' I was surprised. I asked her what she meant, and she shrugged her shoulders. 'Men don't like ambitious women.' According to her, a woman couldn't be a doctor unless she was ambitious. I laughed and agreed that it was probably true. I was thinking of when I first came to London, and certain people had refused to be treated by me. The men I could understand, it was the women who puzzled me. But I hadn't given up, and in the end they had come round. Anyway, both my parents had died when I was very young. I was brought up by an aunt who was also a nurse. She encouraged me to go into medicine, and I had found the work interesting. I was good at it too. So it was the natural thing for me to do.

A commotion started up at the pond. One of the swans reared up and, fanning its wings, paddled across the water towards the children. They screamed and ran away, dropping their stick. The swan moved off and the children resumed their baiting. But the swans kept their distance now and the children soon got bored and drifted off. Once they'd gone Anna turned to me and said, 'That's something we have in common.' I didn't know what she was talking about, so she explained: 'We're both orphans.'

A cloud blocked out the sun and looking up I realised it was late in the day. Anna walked with me to the bus stop and waited until the bus came. In the warmth of the upper deck I watched the city bowl past, the houses shrinking and squeezing closer together. By the time the bus turned into the main road dusk was falling. There was no sign of the bookie, or the man on the soapbox. A few of the local lads were hanging about on a corner. But otherwise the street was deserted, just like every other Sunday evening.

Chapter 5

On my way back from my morning round the next day, I stopped at a café in the main road. I was hungry and I liked the idea of sitting by a window, watching life go past on the street outside. From where I sat I could see the chicken shop opposite. Klamm waved to me from behind the counter. He mouthed something I couldn't understand and patted his paunch. I smiled and waved back.

Just then the café owner came over, wiped the table and took my order. When I turned back to the window I spotted the Rose brothers outside the greengrocer's. Cyril was sitting in a wheelchair beside a stand laden with fruit and vegetables, nodding his head at what he wanted. The greengrocer would pick up a cabbage or a potato, and Cyril would shake his head and demand one from lower down the pile, while the greengrocer shot him resentful glances. Meanwhile Benjamin stood by with the basket over his arm and that same little half smile on his face.

After lunch I took the short cut home and came out by the Salvation Army. A shiny black car was parked by the kerb outside the surgery. There were no markings on it but I could tell it hadn't been there long, because the children were still standing some way off, huddled together, pointing and trying to peer in the windows.

As soon as I stepped into the hall I heard voices. They were coming from my waiting room and I stopped to listen. Some kind of argument was going on. I heard a man say, 'What's that? What's that? Speak up boy.' There was a short silence and then a couple of muffled smacks; then another silence, and a different man's voice said, 'You might as well admit it. It'll be better for you if you do.'

I opened the door. A tall, fair man with a red, blotchy face started towards me with his fists clenched, but the other, who was shorter and almost completely bald, put out his hand to stop him. The balding man smiled at me in an ingratiating way and said, 'You must be the doctor.' His partner dropped his fists and stepped back, looking a bit sheepish. Behind him stood Paul Janowitz. I hadn't noticed him until then. He stood with his head bowed and his shoulders hunched, so that I could hardly see his face. Angrily I asked the balding man what was the meaning of this.

Without relaxing his smile he explained that he and his colleague were policemen. I think he said he was a detective. Anyway, they were investigating the case of the officer who had died after the riot. I didn't say anything, and he went on. He had reason to believe that Paul had been on the barricade that day. Although Paul had denied it he had no alibi. He wanted to know if I could remember anything that might be relevant.

Without thinking I said, 'Yes.' The policemen looked at each other but Paul didn't move. He stood with his chin tucked into his chest. I explained that Paul had come to my surgery at about lunchtime. He had been walking past the main road when he came across a boy lying in the gutter. The boy had been trampled underfoot by the crowd. One of his ribs had been broken. Paul stayed while I bandaged him up and then he took the boy home.

The two officers exchanged glances again. The detective told me I would have to go down to the station to make a statement. I said I would be happy to do so. Then he smiled his ingratiating smile and said, 'Of course, you'll be able to furnish us with the boy's name and address.' After that he turned to Paul and told him that he too would be required to give a statement. Paul raised his head and nodded. There was a red weal under his right eye. He asked if he was free to go. The tall, fair man said, 'For now,' and without looking at me Paul walked past them and out of the room. I heard him climb the stairs. The two men picked up their hats off a chair by the door and just before they left the detective told me I would be notified about giving a statement. A moment later, I heard his partner roaring at the children in the street, telling them to 'scarper'.

I went upstairs and opened the window to let in some air. It had rained during the morning and you could still smell the wetness of the cobbles. Just then there was a knock on the door and Paul came in. I asked him to sit down but he wouldn't. He looked at me and said, 'It wasn't true, what you said.' I shrugged my shoulders, as if to say it didn't matter. And yet I couldn't explain why I had lied, except out of indignation at the police officers' behaviour. He said, 'If they find the boy, he'll tell them I left as soon as you arrived. He'll say it was you who took him home.'

I'd already thought about that. It was just the boy's word against mine. All the same, I felt uncomfortable about it. For the second time in a few days I'd been drawn into someone else's life. I'd taken risks for them. And I only had myself to blame.

Paul looked at the bed in the corner. In my hurry that morning I had forgotten to make it. He looked away quickly and with his fingertips started to rub his cheek. I noticed again how long his nails were. I asked him if the policeman had hit him and to my surprise he laughed. 'Yes,' he said, 'But I'm used to it.' He was smiling, as if it was some kind of game. He added, 'It's because I'm a communist. Whenever there's trouble they come looking for us. They rough a couple of us up, to teach us a lesson, and then they go away again.'

I went into the kitchen and came back with a half bottle of brandy and a glass. I offered him some, but he didn't reply. He was still standing by the door, rubbing his cheek. I sat down at the little wooden table. Paul watched me, but in a sort of preoccupied way, as if he didn't see me. After a while he said that his mother didn't know he was a communist. He didn't want to upset her. 'She's an old woman. She doesn't want any trouble.' I told him I could understand her point of view. He gave me an odd look. Then he said he'd changed his mind: he would sit down after all.

He crossed the room in two strides and without making a sound slid into the chair opposite me. He was wearing a black jacket over a greyish shirt which was buttoned up to the neck. The collar of the shirt was frayed but clean, and the jacket was worn. Facing him across the table I noticed how bad his complexion was. His skin was pale and waxy. His chin was covered in an uneven stubble and there were red pimples showing through it. It was obvious he hadn't been sleeping.

I poured some brandy into the glass and Paul gulped it down, placing the empty glass to one side. We sat in silence for a moment and then, to put him at his ease, I asked about his mother. He suddenly looked sad. Ever since he was a little boy, he told me, he'd been responsible for her. His father had died when he was nine and after that her health had deteriorated very quickly. It had never been good, because of the terrible things they did to her before she and his father left Russia, when she was in the camps.

I told him that local people knew how well he cared for his mother and admired him for it. He seemed pleased. 'I don't mind doing it,' he said, 'because I'm used to it. That's the way it's always been.' But sometimes he found it frustrating, because even though he loved her, he wasn't a free agent. He always had to think about her needs. And yet it was because he loved her, and wanted to avenge the terrible things that had happened to her, that he had become a communist in the first place.

Sitting back in his chair he placed his hands on the table with the fingers spread apart. He didn't mind being 'roughed up' every now and then, he said, because it was for a good cause. But this time it was different, because a policeman had died. Someone would have to pay for that. The police wanted an arrest and a court case. 'It's not that I'm scared,' he said. 'But if I'm arrested, who will look after mother?'

I didn't reply. Paul ran his hand through his hair a couple of times. Then he started to speak very quickly. On the day of the riot, he hadn't gone to work at all. He was on the barricade. He saw the boy from the lorry, not the side street. After he'd brought him to the surgery, he went straight back there. He'd lied for his mother's sake, because it would frighten her to know that he had taken such chances. 'I didn't think it would do any harm,' he said. I told him it made no difference to me. It was none of my business where he was that day. But he rightly pointed out that I had made it my business when I lied to the police.

'Tell me the story from the begining,' I said, after a pause. He took a deep breath. He and his comrades had planned a peaceful protest, and it had started off that way. But when the blackshirts turned back, things got out of hand. People started throwing bricks and bits of rubble, anything they could get their hands on. He didn't join in, because there wasn't any point. The blackshirts had already gone. But he climbed up on the lorry to try and get above it. It was then that he had caught sight of this woman running towards him. 'She was screaming and her hair was standing on end. I think she was some kind of lunatic. People just got out of her way. But I had this idea it was me she wanted and I couldn't take my eyes off her.'

The crowd in front of the lorry surged forward to surround her and he lost sight of her after that. But in the space that opened up behind it he saw the boy lying motionless on the ground. At first he had thought he was dead, but he wasn't. So he'd brought him to me. And then he'd headed straight back to the main road.

The sound of the rain drew our attention to the window and I got up to close it. The water drummed against the glass. I poured some more brandy and Paul drank it. Then he said, 'What happened next, it's bad. Very bad.'

He got up and walked around the room. Then he stopped, looked down at his boots, and as if addressing them, carried on with his story. 'This policeman blocked my path. He wouldn't let me through. He had a baton and he was pointing it at me and cursing. I didn't want any trouble, but he just kept telling me to "back off". And then, suddenly, he just fell down in front of me. He was kneeling at my feet with his head bowed forward, and at the back of his head was this sticky red mess.'

Just then he caught sight of his mate in the crowd. His mate told him to run for it. That's when he realised there was blood everywhere. Some of it had got on his clothes. It looked bad for him, and he got out of there as fast as he could.

We sat in silence and he wouldn't meet my eye. Then he repeated some of the things he'd said earlier. He couldn't risk being arrested because he had to think about his mother; the place was swarming with people and somebody was bound to call an ambulance. When I pointed out that no one had, he looked up with a startled expression. So I told him it was all right, I didn't blame him for the policeman's death. It seemed to me to be one of those situations where no single person was to blame. It was just a tragic accident. He said, 'An accident, yes.'

Outside the rain had stopped and the sky was clearing. I looked at my watch. My waiting room would be filling up with patients. Paul got to his feet. At the door he asked me what I was going to tell the police. 'You could tell them you made a mistake,' he said, 'It's not too late. But if you lie on oath it's perjury. You could go to gaol.'

I thought about it. If I changed my story I would no

longer be involved. But Paul might go to gaol, even though he'd done nothing wrong. Then his mother would suffer. And what good would that do? So I told him he had nothing to worry about; that I liked his mother and would do nothing to hurt her. He looked at me, then bowed his head sharply and left.

I returned the brandy to the kitchen and washed my hands. On my way to the door I caught my reflection in the mirror and turned to face it fully. But nothing in my appearance had changed. So I let myself out of the flat and went downstairs. Outside the Janowitzes' I heard the old lady chattering away in her strange language and Paul saying, 'Yes, mama,' and 'No, mama'. Then, Paul would say a whole sentence in the same language, she would laugh her quavering laugh, and he would laugh too. I listened for a moment, because I wanted to be sure I had made the right decision. Then I carried on down the stairs.

Chapter 6

The following week Anna telephoned to say the stickers were ready. Later that same morning I went to the police station to give my statement. The balding detective led me into a small room with grubby blue walls and no window. There was a table pushed up against the wall, two chairs, and a naked light bulb hanging down from the ceiling. The light bounced off his bald spot and picked out every pore in his nose. From the moment I entered the room I felt like a criminal. At the same time I realised that that was how I was supposed to feel.

He started by questioning me about the boy. He wanted to know everything in minute detail, including the colour of his hair and the number of marbles he'd been carrying. It got on my nerves but when I pointed out that there were patients waiting to see me he smiled his ingratiating smile and said, 'They'll understand. After all, a man is dead.' I almost felt guilty then, as if I was preventing him from bringing a murderer to justice. So I had to remind myself that it was Paul we were talking about, and in fact there was no murderer in this case.

He wanted to know the exact timings of Paul's movements on the day of the riot. I repeated what I had already told him. But after each piece of information he looked up from his pad and said, 'You're certain?' He then thanked me for my cooperation and said he'd like to ask me a few personal questions. That's when I lost my temper. I wanted to know who was the suspect in this case, Paul or me. He smiled again and informed me that it was 'just for the record'. There was no point in getting angry, so I told him what he wanted to know. I signed the statement and he showed me to the door. But as I was walking away he called after me that he'd be in touch. And when I looked back he was still standing there, watching me.

I stopped for lunch at the café in the main road. I had a headache and I didn't feel much like talking. But Klamm came in and sat down at my table. Beads of sweat spotted his forehead and he looked unwell. Before he could speak the café owner came over with my liver and onions, nodded at Klamm and said, 'What'll it be?' Klamm made a face and waved his hand in the air. He couldn't eat because of the pain in his stomach, he said. He was suffering a bad attack of acid. Certain people gave him acid and the acid gave him pain. But the pain was like a warning. It told him a person was no good.

The café owner went back behind the counter and Klamm asked me if the woman who'd got beaten up had found me. I realised he meant Anna and I said, 'Yes.' He looked sheepish. He felt bad about giving her my address, he said, but now he was going to make up for it by passing on a warning. It was because of her that he couldn't eat. 'She's trouble. I knew it as soon as I set eyes on her.' It was always the same with politics, he went on. People who got involved wound up in the gutter. You had to keep your head down and be grateful for what you had. His grandpa knew it and that's why he left Germany and came to England. 'Out of respect for the old man I keep my hands clean.'

His wife appeared in the doorway, wiping her hands on her apron. She wanted to know if he was going to leave her in the shop all day long. Then she saw me and said, 'Stop bothering the doctor.' He got to his feet and announced that he had to get back. But before he went, he had one more thing to say to me. He just wanted me to know that sensitive stomachs ran in his family. His father had had one, and so had his grandpa. 'And they were never wrong yet.'

I took the long way home. The men who passed me in the street had removed their jackets and rolled up their sleeves, and the young women seemed to float along in thin cotton dresses. The sun beat down on my bare arms and I walked along under a summer sky. My headache had gone and the thought of Klamm and his stomach made me smile. When I got home I went straight into the surgery and saw the six or seven patients who were waiting for me. As soon as the last one had gone, I set out to see Cyril Rose.

I hadn't paid Cyril a visit since Benjamin came to the surgery, and I didn't know what to expect. Benjamin opened the door, and to my surprise he seemed overjoyed to see me. He led me into the parlour and there was Cyril, awake and brighter than I had seen him in months. He smiled and told me that he had woken up that morning with no pain. According to him, it was a 'miracle' and he couldn't remember the last time it had happened. I was pleased but I didn't want him to get his hopes up. So I warned him that it might only be temporary. He nodded and said it was a miracle all the same. When Benjamin showed me out he didn't speak. I smiled at him and when he took my hand there were tears in his eyes.

It was still light outside and the air was warm. The moon was already hanging large and pale in the sky. Children were playing in the street and men were drifting home from work with their jackets slung over their shoulders and cigarettes hanging out of their mouths. From the pub on the opposite corner came the sound of clinking glasses and laughter. Everything seemed simple and good, and I strolled along in no hurry to get home.

Around eight there was a knock on my door and Paul came in. He wanted to know how it had gone at the police station. I told him that I'd kept to my story, but I couldn't guarantee that the detective had believed me. He looked relieved all the same. I then remarked that after this morning I could understand how innocent people confessed to crimes they hadn't committed. He laughed and said, 'That's policemen for you,' and then he left.

Gradually the sounds of the city died. I made coffee and sat down to face the window. At half past eleven the house was quiet and I was standing in darkness, looking down into the yard. Anna was late. The thought crossed my mind that she had decided not to come after all. If so I would go to bed and my life would carry on as normal. But I couldn't help feeling disappointed. I lingered by the window and after a few minutes she appeared on the wall that separated the yard from the narrow alley behind. There was a wooden door in the wall, that opened inwards, but the hinges must have rusted. Considering her small size, I was struck by how nimbly she climbed. She was wearing black slacks and a pullover, and she landed with both feet on Mrs Janowitz's sofa, whose springs groaned beneath her weight. Perhaps she thought it had been left there as junk, because she didn't seem surprised to see it. She simply headed for the entrance to the building, which I had left unlocked.

As I waited for her, I felt a swirling in my stomach. I was grateful for the darkness, even though I was in my own flat. Once again I was thinking like a criminal, and yet I hadn't done anything wrong. I was only going to post some stickers. That's what I told myself and yet it made no difference. Each time I swallowed it left a bad taste in my mouth.

As soon as Anna arrived I felt better. Then the whole thing became an adventure, thrilling and at the same time farcical. She had instructed me to dress inconspicuously, and after looking me up and down she nodded her approval. I was glad I had remembered to wear my soft-soled shoes, so my feet would make no noise on the cobbles. A black canvas bag lay against her hip and the strap sloped across her bosom. Removing a sticker from the bag she demonstrated how to conceal it in the palm of the hand and swipe it across the chosen surface.

As we were about to leave, she produced a flask, unscrewed the lid, jerked her head back sharply to swig from it, and passed it to me. For a second the metal gleamed in the moonlight, and then it was alcohol swirling in my stomach, and I no longer felt nervous. Anna slapped me on the back and said, 'Let's go.'

I had drawn a map in my head, and we worked slowly northwards, keeping to the back streets. Anna did one side while I did the other. There was nobody about, apart from the shadows that flitted along the walls, waiting just long enough for us to turn a corner before they vanished round the next, or dissolved altogether. There were sounds too, as of men brawling underground, or rats rummaging in garbage. Passing one alleyway, I turned my head to face a pair of steady eyes, cool gold, puncturing the darkness. I couldn't tell if it was a distant dog or a rat up close, but then the blackness snuffed them out and there was the rhythmic padding of feet. A fox trotted past me, leaning into the wall, then vanished again into the shadows.

At the corner of Fournier Street I stopped, thinking I had taken a wrong turn. But it was just that the sewing machines were quiet and I hardly recognised the place without them. I slapped a sticker on the wall and moved on, heading south again by a different route. We had only been gone a couple of hours but it seemed longer. I kept expecting the dawn to break. The air was cold and clean, and the buildings were clean too, as if the night had whitewashed the smoke-blackened walls, swept up the guano from the pigeon coops, and removed the rags from the broken window panes. In the moonlight none of the streets looked the same.

Crossing one street we entered another which ran perpendicular, and I had a feeling of déjà vu. I couldn't shake the idea that Anna and I were once again the only human beings on the planet. We skirted the pools of light cast by the streetlamps, groping for smooth surfaces, and as we felt our way around my fingers observed something that my eyes had missed, which was that there were very few clear surfaces left. Most were already encrusted with posters and bills and stickybacks. The lamp posts were swaddled in them, and in places the walls were spongy to the touch, as if they were made of papier mâché, and a single match would send the whole lot up in flames.

It occurred to me then that if I had not noticed the slogans screaming out from the walls, perhaps no one else had either, and that the only people who pay attention to posters are those who post them. That's when I began to enjoy myself, because I realised how insignificant it all was. By that time we had almost come full circle and it was impossible to believe that we could be caught or seen. We even ventured out into the main road, keeping close to the walls, and fixed our stickers to the brick between the shopfronts.

Anna took the north side while I took the south. Ahead of me, in the distance, I could make out the bright lights of the Pavilion, silent and deserted, and the Vapour Baths with its ghostly glow around the entrance. I didn't like to think of the Vapour Baths existing at night, empty and deep and still. I was still gazing at it when I felt Anna's hand on my arm. She was breathing hard, as if she had been running, and her eyes glittered in the light from the distant theatre. She held open her bag to indicate that there were no more stickers. Neither of us said anything. We had agreed that there was no point in staying together longer than was necessary, and a minute later she vanished.

I walked home slowly, listening to my echoing footsteps and wondering why I had felt so nervous about posting a few stickers. It seemed ridiculous now. I slept well and when I woke the next morning the sky beyond the window was full of seagulls, wheeling and shrieking. I couldn't be sure if the previous night's escapade had really happened, or if I had dreamt it. I soon realised it was real, but just to be sure, I went out to see if anything had changed. As I emerged into the street the first thing I saw was a boy coming towards me along the pavement. He had dirty scabs on his knees and he was trailing a stick along the fronts of the buildings, making a loud scraping noise and looking straight at me with an insolent expression.

From then on everyone I saw seemed to be performing some activity involving walls. A drunk lay across the pavement, his head and one shoulder propped against the wall. Above the fishmonger's a woman with a scarf wrapped tightly round her head peered out from a hole in the wall to chat to someone below. A little further on a man on a stepladder pasted an advertisement for a circus over some bills advertising Brooke Bond tea. Here and there I spotted one of my own stickers, but it was as if they were invisible. People went about their lives, moving easily in and out of walls, and pretending all the time that they weren't there.

By the evening, I had forgotten all about it. Morris came round and announced that he was taking me up west. His hair was greased back and he was wearing a white shirt with a starched collar under his Sunday jacket. I put on my grey crêpe dress and he called me a 'vision'. I asked him if that was a compliment and he laughed. We went to a Chinese restaurant and ate octopus and drank tea with flowers in it. The restaurant was packed with gay people and so were the streets. Everybody seemed to be celebrating and when I told Morris he said he'd noticed it too. According to him, it was human nature, because any day now we would be at war.

After dinner we went to a music hall. It was a variety show and at the side of the stage a girl in a sparkling dress flipped a deck of cards to show the number of the act. One was called 'Scenes From Apache Life' and then there was a magician. I enjoyed his tricks, even though a lot of them were old. But Morris preferred the finale, which was a line of girls in tights performing the cancan. When the show was over, we went to a pub and drank gin. And then, because neither of us felt tired, we went to a club and drank some more gin and danced.

At three in the morning we took a taxi home. Morris asked me to marry him and this time, he said, it was official. I pointed out that he was going away. 'You may feel differently when you come back.' But he insisted that could never happen. Besides, nothing had been decided and he was very happy in his work. If I preferred, though, we could wait a year until it was all over. I smiled and kissed him. From then on neither of us spoke. The motion of the car lulled me into a sort of trance. The bright lights of the city poured past the window in a more or less constant stream. Watching them rain down on the wind-screen and cascade off to either side, I had the impression that they were bullets, and the taxi was carrying Morris and me into battle.

The next day, Sunday, Morris and I heard the news together. It was announced on the wireless: the country was at war. Neither of us spoke but Morris held my hand tightly. My head ached and my mouth felt dry. I tried to understand what it meant. Would there be guns in the streets? Would we starve? But although a calamity was about to overwhelm us I couldn't imagine how my life would change.

A bit later, Anna phoned. She asked me to come over. I told her I had company but she insisted it was important. It had to do with the other night. I asked her if something had happened but she said she couldn't discuss it over the phone. So I agreed. I told Morris it was a medical emergency, because I don't think he would have understood. When I got to the restaurant, I found it closed and dark. I tried the door but it was locked. I was just wondering what to do when a man appeared from a door at the side. He had curly dark hair and his tie was askew. He was carrying his jacket over his arm. Glancing at me, he set off across the street, but before he had got half way a window sash rattled up above us. It was Anna. She was wearing a blue silk dressing gown over a lacy nightdress which gaped at the chest. She called out to him, but I didn't catch his name. Holding the sash with one hand she blew him a kiss, then disappeared back inside.

The man and I looked at each other. I smiled politely, but he just frowned and stormed off. I watched him go, then stepped up to the door that he had just come out of. It was open. I called to Anna and she shouted, 'Come in!' A moment later I was in her bedroom. She was sitting with her short legs crossed on the bed, an ashtray brimming with cigarette butts in her lap, smoking. The bed was unmade and clothes were scattered about the floor. In the corner by the window stood a dummy with a half made dress on it, held together by pins. Anna wasn't wearing her scarf as usual, and I noticed that the bruise had gone. But there was an ugly red scar on her temple, like a worm wriggling across it.

She patted the bed and I sat down. I told her I had come as quickly as I could and she leaned forward, kissing me on both cheeks. We looked at each other and she asked me if I'd seen the man in the street. I nodded and she wanted to know if I had found him 'good-looking'. All I could remember was his angry expression, so I shrugged my shoulders. 'His name's Val Nolan,' she announced. 'He's my lover.'

She'd only known him three days. He'd come into the restaurant a couple of times and they'd got talking. The night before, for the first time, she'd let him make love to her. I didn't say anything and she wanted to know if I was shocked. I said, 'No', because things like that didn't shock me. Some expression passed across her face and I thought perhaps she was disappointed. But it was only a fleeting look and when I asked her who he was she didn't hesitate. 'He's a brave man and a hero.'

There was a short silence while she drew on her cigarette. I asked her if she had heard the news. But she didn't seem to understand. 'What news?' So I explained about the war and she said, 'Oh that.' She frowned and waved her hand, so that the cigarette smoke wafted up to my nostrils. 'That doesn't mean a thing.'

I was puzzled. I had assumed that she would be upset. So I asked her why she had wanted to see me. She looked at me with an odd expression and then she held up her half-smoked cigarette. 'See this?' she said. But before I could answer she had stabbed the glowing end on to the back of her hand. She held it there for a few seconds, then uttered a cry and removed it. A black and red circle of burned skin remained.

I was horrified and I demanded to why she had done it. She just laughed. It was to show me that it took more than a little pain to put her off, she said. Torture was something she knew all about. She had seen how the communists treated their prisoners and it didn't frighten her. She would keep fighting until they were broken, and the small matter of the declaration of war wouldn't stop her. 'After all,' she added, 'No bombs have fallen yet, have they?'

She was holding her injured hand out level, as if to let the air cool it, and I asked her to let me clean the wound. But she shook her head. Leaning over she kissed me again. 'You're my friend,' she said, smiling. With her good hand, she removed another cigarette from the pack lying beside her, and then she started talking again. The reason she had asked me to come over, she said, was to let me know that she hadn't given up. Her lover had a plan and he wanted her to help him carry it out. She couldn't tell me anything about it, not yet, but this time it would be far more daring. She had just wanted to let me know so that I wouldn't 'lose hope'.

She paused to light the cigarette and I noticed that her hand shook. I felt very sorry for her, but now more as a doctor feels sorry for a patient she can no longer help. An idea obsessed her and she couldn't see beyond it. I had no desire to be drawn into her plan and I told her I had to go. She said, 'Yes. But we'll be seeing each other again.' The tone of her voice was cold, as if she was issuing a command. And yet she was still smiling. I left her and walked back towards the river, wondering how things had changed, and what would happen next.

Chapter 7

There was a war on but people got ill in the usual way. I was busy all week and Morris came round on Friday. The next morning he jumped out of bed and threw up the window. The sun glinted off the rooftops and he said we were enjoying what was called an Indian summer. I suggested that we go down to the river and he kissed me. He had things to do, he said, but he'd come back later and we'd go for a picnic. I'd buy the food and he'd bring the booze. We'd go to the jetty.

As soon as he had gone I had a visitor. It was Anna. She was wearing a black beret instead of the usual coloured scarf. She sat down in the armchair and looked at me. I kept my eyes fixed on her and waited to hear what she had to say. But she took her time. First she fished a pack of cigarettes out of her jacket pocket and asked me if there was anything to drink. I went into the kitchen and came back with the brandy. I poured two glasses and took a sip. She downed hers in one.

She started talking about the stickers. According to her, it had been a complete waste of time. I'd known that all along but I didn't say anything. She added, 'It was wrong of me to drag you into it.' I replied, I don't know why, that I had been glad to help her out. She said, 'All the same, it was wrong.' She smoked her cigarette, staring at the floor. Then, as if the idea had just occurred to her, she announced there was something she wanted to show me. It meant walking a little way and she couldn't tell me anything beforehand. I would just have to trust her on it.

I asked her what it was all about but she just shook her head and smiled. So I told her I didn't think I'd come. I'd helped her as much as I could and besides, I was waiting for someone. According to her it wouldn't take more than half an hour. It was very important and she appealed to me as a friend. Then she repeated what she had said before: that I would have to trust her on it. I still didn't feel like going, but she promised it would be the last thing she'd ask me to do. We left immediately, but down in the hall, she instructed me to follow her at a discreet distance.

There were no children in the street. They had all left the city and now that they'd gone the place sounded different: hollow and wintry. It was as if the Pied Piper had been through and lured them all away. I was walking along and thinking this and then I saw that up ahead of me Anna was dressed like a man. I hadn't noticed it before. She was wearing slacks and a dark jacket that was too broad in the shoulder, the beret and a red handkerchief knotted round her neck.

She was heading into a bad part of the neighbourhood. I had visited some of those houses and they were infested with rats and insects. That was in the summer. In the winter they were damp. Many of them were brothels. I was surprised because she seemed to know where she was going, but then I remembered something she'd said: the place where she was taking me she had been to once before.

On a narrow, street overshadowed by a factory wall she stopped at a door and looked around her. I was still about fifty yards away and there was no one else in sight. She knocked on the door, but in a special way, in some kind of code. As I walked towards her I saw her lean towards the closed door and say something into it. A moment later I reached her and we both entered at the same time. A young man who had been standing behind the door closed it quietly and showed us down a short passage and into a room.

The room was dark and full of cigarette smoke. It felt cluttered and I was aware of other people. A man was talking. At first I couldn't see much but gradually my eyes grew accustomed to the gloom. At the far end the man who was talking sat at a table with his back to me. He had dark curly hair and I recognised Val Nolan. He was holding a pair of headphones to his head and in his right hand, clamped between his fingers, was a burnt down cigarette. As I watched a stack of ash fell off under its own weight and drifted to the floor.

The walls of the room were piled high with books and old newspapers. To Nolan's right the wall was entirely covered in newspaper cuttings and a young woman was busy pasting new ones up over the old. Besides her there were a couple of other young people, lounging round and smoking. One of them, who was squatting on the floor, looked up at Anna and nodded. Nobody spoke. But then the young man who had let us in came up to Anna and whispered something in her ear. He handed her a slim package wrapped in brown paper. She slipped it into her jacket pocket. Nolan was still talking. He spoke very loudly and clearly, in English, and yet he wasn't making any sense. For instance, there was something about a big man being wrapped in paper and damp matches in Surrey. I guessed it was some kind of code, but there was no time to think about it because Anna came over and told me it was time to leave. I was to go first, and take a different route home. She would follow me shortly, and meet me back at the flat.

It was good to be outside again in the fresh air. I cut down an alleyway and came out in a courtyard by the back door of a factory. There was some kind of row going on. A man was standing in the doorway, shaking his head and gesticulating. Around him was a little group of men who were shouting angrily and waving brown envelopes in his face, at the same time keeping their distance and not touching him. I recognised some of them and I knew immediately what was going on. Every Saturday the supervisor distributed the wages and the machinists complained they were short. So the supervisor told them, 'You don't like it, you leave.' It was all piecework anyway. But the factories were all the same, the supervisor knew it and the men knew it. So they came back, and worked quietly all week, knowing their wages would be short, until Saturday when the same thing happened all over again. It was a ritual and nothing changed it. Not even a war.

Turning the corner into my own street I almost collided with Paul Janowitz. He hurried past without saying anything. A moment later I saw another man walking towards me. He looked familiar and when I got closer I recognised the balding detective. He didn't seem surprised to see me. He merely raised his hat and walked on past. It struck me as odd, but I decided not to get involved. The surgery came into sight and my thoughts turned back to Anna.

As soon as she arrived I poured us both a brandy and then I asked her straight out what was in the packet. But she shook her head. First she wanted to explain about Nolan. She started speaking in a breathless way. The place where we had just been was the headquarters of an underground radio station. It was his idea, to rally 'the faithful': all those who knew this was a communist war and it wasn't too late to stop it. But the only way to do so now was to wait for the German liberation. So he'd had the bright idea of broadcasting coded messages to all those who stood firm, telling them how to prepare for the invasion. The brown paper packet contained stickybacks advertising the frequency, and it was Anna's job to post them.

We looked at each other. A thought occurred to me, and it was the same thought I had had when I first met her: that she had come from a long way away, and was heading for a distant place. In the meantime our paths had crossed, and now we were about to part again. She was still looking at me, waiting for me to speak. So I said, 'Isn't that a form of treason?' and she laughed out loud. She seemed proud of it.

There was another pause. I had an idea that she was going to ask me to help her. But perhaps I was wrong. I'll never know anyway, because just then I heard Morris whistling a tune as he climbed the stairs. He came into the room backwards, because his hands were full with a cardboard box. When he saw Anna he smiled and said, 'Hello, there.' She blushed and smiled back. I introduced her, and he put the box down saying he'd brought beer and a bottle of wine. It was packed in newspaper to keep it cool.

He seemed very cheerful and then he said he had an announcement to make. 'I bumped into my boss. He called me "son" and he bought me a beer.' Anyone who worked at the factory knew that if the boss called you 'son' that was a sure sign. It meant a promotion or at the very least a pay rise. The war was going to put a lot of work his boss's way and the factory would be at full stretch. So now we had a reason to celebrate and since Anna was there we also had the perfect excuse. 'Three's a party,' he said, grinning at her. Anna laughed and blushed again. I could tell she liked him. She started to say something about getting back to the restaurant and I told Morris we mustn't keep her. But he refused to let her go. For one afternoon, he said, we were going to forget about the war and have a good time.

The three of us set off. In the main road we stopped to buy provisions: salt beef, bread, sardines, a tin of sandwich spread and some chocolate. More beer and some paper cups. We needed something to cut the food with but Anna said she had the solution to that problem, and she pulled a small sheath knife out of her pocket. It had been her father's, she said, turning it over in the palm of her hand. Morris teased her, saying, 'You're a bandit. You're even dressed like one.'

We headed for the river, passing through the little square where the bird fair was held. It was in full swing, but there was no sign of the boy with the mynah bird and there were fewer cages than usual. I walked ahead, leading the way with the food, and Morris and Anna walked behind, Morris carrying the cardboard box. On the way he entertained her with stories about his boss and things that had happened at the factory.

There was nobody on the jetty, as usual, but the sun sparkled on the little waves and the seagulls wheeled and dived. Down on the shore two men in waders were trudging along, their heads bent, occasionally stooping to pick something off the mud and place it in the nets they had slung over their shoulders. The surface of the mud was like a rubbish tip, scattered with old bits of furniture, shoes, dead birds and something that looked like the skull of a small animal. It seemed a strange pastime, but then again, it was pleasant down there by the water.

The sun was warm and with the brandy already inside me I felt content and a little sleepy. We laid out the picnic and started eating. The food tasted good. Anna was in high spirits and I was glad she had come after all. She told a story about some 'loudmouthed yankees' who had come into her restaurant the night before. They had been drunk and one of the women had complained about her food. She didn't like the sauce. So to teach her some manners Anna had taken it back into the kitchen, removed the sauce, drenched it in gravy browning, old coffee grounds and vinegar, then spat in it for good measure, and returned it to the table. It still made her smile to think of it.

Morris took out his handkerchief, knotted it at the corners, and arranged it on his head. Anna laughed, and he ordered her to remove her red one and did the same with it. I lay back on the rough boards and closed my eyes. I must have dozed off because when I woke up Anna and Morris were sitting side by side with their backs to me, dangling their legs off the end of the jetty. They had both rolled up their trousers to the knee, even though the water was far below, and removed their jackets. Anna was wearing a short-sleeved white shirt and Morris had rolled his sleeves up to his elbows. They were chatting but I couldn't hear what they were saying. Morris was throwing pieces of gravel up into the air so that they landed in the water with a splash. Through my half-open eyes his hair looked white and merged with the handkerchief and the sky beyond. But beside him Anna stood out with her red handkerchief on her dark hair.

I closed my eyes and when I opened them again nobody was talking. Morris was bending over me, stroking my bare legs with his fingers. He was smiling and brushing his fingers up and down, very lightly, pushing them a bit further up under my dress each time. It made my skin tingle. There was a light breeze blowing and I could hardly distinguish it from his touch. Then he leant over and kissed me and his mouth was cool against mine. Anna was asleep, lying back on the jetty with her legs still dangling over the edge.

Morris made a gesture and we both got to our feet. Neither of us spoke. We walked for a little way along the river, clinging tightly to each other and walking in step, until we came to a tumbledown old warehouse. A narrow wooden door had been left ajar. There was nobody about, but when we ventured inside we came face to face with the boxing ring where The Kid had won his fight. We looked at each other and laughed, because of all the warehouses we could have chosen it seemed like fate had led us to that one. Of course it was nothing more than a coincidence, but at that moment I felt closer to

Morris than ever before. I knew how lonely I would be if he went away.

When we got back to the jetty, Anna was awake and finishing off the last of the beer. She watched us walk towards her with a thoughtful expression. We packed up the remains of the picnic and set off home. When we reached the little square Anna said she wanted to have a look at the birds. She thought she'd like to have some for the restaurant. 'Two lovebirds in a cage,' she said, smiling at Morris. Morris announced that he would escort her in, and arm in arm they disappeared into the little avenue of cages. But I stayed outside, because I remembered what had happened last time.

I was wandering up and down, listening to the chatter of the birds, when I caught sight of Paul. He was crossing the square, walking away from me in the direction of the river. He hadn't seen me. When I called to him he hesitated, then looked over his shoulder and walked very quickly towards me. Suddenly he stopped and a sort of frozen look came over his face. He was staring at me and I couldn't understand what was the matter with him. But before I could call out a strange sound came from behind me, as if somebody was being strangled. I turned to see Anna standing at the entrance of the bird market. Her lips were drawn back over her teeth like an animal, and her hair seemed to stand on end. She was looking past me at Paul.

After that everything happened very fast and I couldn't make sense of it. I remember Anna running and how I put out a hand to stop her. But it was no good and the next thing I saw was a flash of metal near her waist. There was a struggle that seemed to go on for a long time, although in reality it must have been over very quickly; the red handkerchief on the cobbles, and Morris shouting from somewhere behind me.

The birds must have sensed that something was wrong because they took fright in their cages and the square was filled with the sound of flapping wings. But of course they couldn't escape and I just had a sense of barely contained movement out of the corner of my eye. The wooden cages clattered against each other and there was a strong smell of guano, stirred up by the great sweeping of air. Above it all, my ears picked out the pure, high tsooeet of a linnet.

Then the balding detective was there. He appeared from nowhere, and his partner too: the tall, fair man with the mottled complexion. I saw them running towards Paul and Anna but their footsteps were drowned out by the deafening noise of the birds. The detective's hat flew off. Watching it float back down to the cobbles, everything became clear in my mind. Paul was the man Anna had seen on the barricade that day. She was the woman who had run like a maniac towards him. Beyond that, I understood that in some way I was to blame for what was happening. I couldn't explain it, it was just a feeling I had. Like the beating of air on my eardrums.

And then it was all over. Anna was kneeling on the cobbles and the tall, fair man was standing behind her, slotting the cuffs on her wrists. The detective held the knife with the blood glistening on its blade. Paul stood a couple of feet away from him, staring down at Anna with that same mesmerised expression, and clutching his arm where the jacket was torn and the shirt beneath it stained red. And above it all, like a voice from another world, was the pure, high tsooeet of a linnet.

PART TWO

Chapter 8

When I woke up I remembered that I was going to a funeral. So I put on a black dress and black shoes. I didn't have a black hat, but I had a bag. In it I kept a pocket torch, with a paper cone to shroud the beam, in case I got caught in the blackout, and a little white flag for waving down buses.

As I set off I noticed that spring had come at last. There was a fresh salt tang to the air, and the sky was a very pale blue, the colour of melted ice. Clouds scudded across the top of it like white horses, and the gulls flew higher than usual, as if the air itself had expanded and thinned out, and there was less of it to weigh them down. Beneath them hung the barrage balloons, like a plague of thunderflies.

Some of the sandbags in the main road had sprouted grass. Others had split, spilling their contents so that in places it was like walking on carpet. At the corner an old man was kicking at the sand and calling to his dog, whose nose was buried in the makeshift wall. The old man looked up at me as I passed and I smiled. I thought I'd seen him before, but I couldn't be sure. Further on a rat oozed its bloated body out of a crevice between two sandbags. It paused for a moment on the pavement, then disappeared into an alley. Watching it go, it occurred to me that if the war didn't get us, the rats would.

A little crowd had gathered outside the chicken shop,

but the shop itself was boarded up. When I asked a woman what had happened she told me that Klamm and his wife had been arrested. The police had come the night before and taken them away in a van. Some other families had gone too: the Keiners from the bakery and the Altmans. I asked her why and she shrugged her shoulders. But a man pointed at the wall to one side of the shop. 'That's why,' he said in a loud voice. He had pointed to a sticker peeling off the wall. It was one of the ones I had posted with Anna. But I couldn't believe I was to blame. The stickers were invisible, no one had taken any notice of them until now.

The group huddled round the sticker and I walked on. Benjamin stood at the church door, greeting the mourners. For the first time I noticed that he was an old man. He seemed thinner and more translucent. He turned his head stiffly and his cheeks hung in papery folds. Throughout the service he stood very dignified and erect and afterwards he thanked me for coming. Cyril was in a better place now, he said. His head had been full of demons but where he had gone they could not follow. I asked him if he was eating properly and his face twisted into a bitter smile. That was all he had to do these days, he said. As I was leaving he called after me. 'You're always welcome, doctor, if you're passing.'

I took the long way home, winding through the back-streets, because the funeral and the news about Klamm had left me feeling sombre. Besides, it was nice to be out in the sun, even if there was not much warmth in it yet. As I did so I paid special attention to the walls. After the long winter the damp had got behind the posters and peeled them away in great swollen tongues. Sodden wads had slid down the lamp posts too, collecting like wrinkled stockings at the bottom. The slogans were no longer legible, except where the old layers had been overlaid with new. For instance, the colourful ones which read, 'Careless Talk Costs Lives.' Only in one or two places did I see the words 'War Destroys Workers', and those had faded almost to nothing.

I felt a bit better and I stopped at Samuel Stores to buy bread. Samuel was leaning on the counter, pulling at his beard and talking to a plump woman whose bosom sagged to her waist. They both turned to look at me, then resumed their conversation. Samuel was talking about a man who had been in some trouble the night before. According to him, this man had recently taken up pipe smoking. He would walk down the street at night, drawing on his pipe until it glowed, and pointing it at the night sky. But the local gang had been watching him and realised that he was sending signals. They'd taken matters into their own hands and 'sorted him out'. He'd be lucky if he ever walked again.

The woman gasped and Samuel shook his beard. 'Bad business,' he said. I took my bread up to the counter and asked if there was any news about Klamm. Samuel told me he hadn't heard anything. Sometimes the police arrested people for no good reason, he said. But in the circumstances, you couldn't blame them. All he knew was that Klamm had always kept himself to himself. 'You don't know which way the wind blows with him.'

The woman nodded. She said, 'It's the quiet ones you've got to look out for.' She asked me how I had found him as a patient. But I told her I wasn't interested in gossip. Samuel gave me my change and I left the shop. By now I was eager to get home and change out of my funeral clothes.

Turning the corner into my road, I saw a large black car parked outside the surgery. It was unusual to see cars since petrol had become so scarce, and I was surprised. On the opposite side of the road three lads were squatting or lounging against the railings. Two of them turned to look at me while the third stared at two men standing by my front door. The men wore police uniforms and my first thought was that they had come to take Paul away. So I quickened my step to intercept them before he opened the door. As I approached another man climbed out of the car. It was the balding detective. Just then one of the officers turned to face me and pulled a card from his pocket. He asked my name, and if I resided at this address, and then he told me that I was under arrest.

He read out something from the card but it didn't mean anything to me. He mentioned some regulations and the word offence, or perhaps defence. I looked at the detective but he just stared back at me with a blank expression. I said, 'There must be some mistake,' but nobody heard. So I said it again, louder, and this time I was sure they were ignoring me. The officer told me to get into the car and that I needn't bring anything. Perhaps I hesitated, or glanced at the door of the building, because he took a step towards me and said, 'Come just as you are,' and there was a threatening note in his voice. I couldn't understand what was happening, and my mind went blank.

I stooped to climb into the car and he followed me in,

while the other policeman took the driver's seat. The detective stayed behind, but I only realised that later. We moved off very quickly, as if in a chase, and as the empty streets and dark, helpless buildings spun past me the thought entered my head that it was the weekend, and you couldn't arrest people on a weekend.

Then a whole series of fantastic ideas came to me, each more improbable than the last. I imagined, for instance, that Morris was playing some kind of practical joke on me, and when we got to our destination he would appear grinning. Or that I was being kidnapped and taken to a secret location where an important prisoner lay hidden. He was suffering from a fever, and because his captors couldn't let him die, or risk having him recognised, they had chosen me to treat him.

The car drew up at a large wooden gate reinforced by iron bolts. Cricking my neck to look out of the window I saw a fortress towering above me, with a jumble of crenellated towers and narrow barred windows. Either side of the gate were two large crucifixes, and I realised that these were windows too, but not for looking out of. The gates opened and the car eased through them into a courtyard. 'This is it,' said the policeman beside me, 'The women's prison.' The way he said it implied that being a woman was reason enough to be there, and his words had the effect of banishing all my fantasies. I knew then that I was really under arrest, that I was going to have a fight on my hands.

Climbing out of the car I noticed there were triangular flowerbeds in the angles between the towers, but nothing had been planted in them, as if to emphasise the fact that this was a prison. Or perhaps nothing could grow there, because too little light filtered down between the walls. I had a sense that the building went back forever, and by stepping through the door I was embarking on a long journey. At the same time I thought that this was how I was supposed to feel.

Inside the prison there was a flurry of activity. A small group of women was gathered there, and from their gesticulations I could tell they were either angry or frightened. Some were shrieking in German, others in English, and what the latter were saying was: I have done nothing wrong, you cannot keep me here. I noticed they used the words I and me, as if none of the others existed. They were being marshalled into a passage by a number of women in grey who kept telling them to 'settle down'. One of these detached herself from the group and came over to me. She started to say something, but I couldn't hear because of the din. She pointed to the receding backs of the women and I realised I was to follow them. I thought about refusing, but judging by her expression, there was no point.

Looking at her I was struck by how ugly she was. Her face was round with creases in it, a ball of putty smeared anticlockwise by a giant's thumb. Her mouth was lopsided, and one nostril was closed so that it whistled when she breathed. She followed me down the passage and we emerged into another room. That's when I noticed that I was still carrying the bread I had bought in Samuel Stores. The wardress tried to take it from me, but I explained that I had paid for it, and therefore it was mine. She took it anyway, along with my bag, and handed me a vast, white calico garment with holes for the neck and arms. 'Take off all your clothes,' she said, indicating a row of cubicles, 'Except for your underwear.'

Over her shoulder I caught sight of a tall, elegant woman with beetle-black eyebrows. Gold bracelets hung loosely from her wrists and she was unclasping them one by one, dangling them from her fingertips, and watching them coil into a cardboard box. Her wrists moved gracefully over one another and the wardress who held the box eyed them greedily. Every so often she shook it as if panning for gold, and then she said the name Roschowski. The tall woman corrected her, rolling the R slightly and shifting the emphasis. Her face was regal and calm, and for some reason I could not take my eyes off her. I stood gazing out from the cubicle until the wardress ordered me to wait there for the doctor, and shut the door.

Inside the wooden box there was barely space to turn around. But I got undressed and pulled the white gown over my head. It was soft and greasy to the touch, and it fell to my ankles emitting a cloud of stale sweat. It occurred to me that this must be what a corpse feels like, shut in a coffin, wearing only a shroud. I sat down on a wooden ledge. Whichever way I sat, my knees jammed against the door. The room beyond was quiet, and I was aware of bodies in other cubicles, shifting listlessly and bumping against the partitions. Someone was snivelling, and from the distance came the reverberating crash of metal, as if a knight in heavy armour were approaching with slow footsteps.

Squares of grey dappled my lap from the wire-meshed roof of the box, but barring the peephole in the door there was no other source of light. Through the gloom I could make out graffiti etched into the dirty, cream-painted walls, but I couldn't read the words and I lost track of time. After what seemed like hours the bolt was thrown back and the lopsided wardress appeared. She was carrying a plate with a hunk of bread on it and a mug of tea. The mug had no handle. Before I could say anything the door slammed shut and I heard the bolt drawn back on the next cubicle.

Suddenly I knew that I couldn't let her go, so I placed the mug and plate on the floor, clenched my fist and thumped on the door as hard as I could. There was no response so I thumped again and a gravelly voice shouted, 'Quiet there!' By the sound of it she had reached the end of the row. The last bolt slid back into place and her footsteps receded. But I started beating on the door again and shouting at the top of my voice. Minutes passed before I became aware that there were splinters in my hand, and I stopped.

Soon after that the doctor came. She was quite young, she wore a white coat, and her long, red-varnished nails peeped round the back of her clipboard like tiny licks of flame. She looked at my grazed knuckles and then at me, but she didn't say anything. She just ticked a box on her clipboard and told me to lift the gown. I didn't move and she repeated her command, but more aggressively this time. It was the rules, she said. She had to check for lice and VD. I explained that I was a doctor, too, and that would not be necessary. Perhaps I expected her to bend the rules for a colleague. But she just looked at me coldly, with something like disgust, and said, 'I don't care. Lift the gown.'

It occurred to me that she had no idea who I was, or why I was there, and neither did the lopsided wardress. Both were following orders from above, and it would be useless to ask for an explanation. The doctor examined me and then ordered me to take a bath. But I had already bathed that morning. In that case, she said, I should skip it and put on my uniform. She pointed to a pile of folded clothes on a trolley behind her. But I didn't want to put the uniform on. To me, that would be admitting defeat. So I asked her politely if I could have my own clothes returned to me. With a malicious smile she said it was too late for that. My clothes had already been 'bagged and tagged'. So unless I wanted to stay in the gown, I might as well do as I was told.

She moved on to the next cubicle, and as there was no alternative I picked up the pile of clothes. The skirt and cardigan were navy blue and both were worn and patched. The heavy black lace-ups had been moulded to other feet. Putting them on I felt a subtle change come over me, as if I had confessed some crime, or taken on the personality of the last person to discard them. Of course I had done nothing of the kind. But when a wardress ordered me to walk ahead of her, I obeyed, following her directions and advancing through endless corridors and doors. It made me feel uneasy, as when walking down an unlit pavement at night you hear foot-steps close behind. Several times I was tempted to step aside and let her pass.

After what seemed like a long time we reached the centre of the prison. Looking up I saw I was in a vast hall of latticed ironwork, spiral staircases and confusing sounds, like an over-populated doll's house with the façade removed, or a cross-section of a termite mound. Cell blocks radiated out from it in a star shape. Standing at the bottom I could see straight up through the netted tiers to the roof of the prison tower. There were no windows, no natural light, and because my eyes weren't used to the gloom it seemed to me to be foggy there. Yellow bulbs burned haloes through the mist and the air was still and cold. It was as if I had descended to an underground city, or a mine.

From the centre I climbed several flights of steps and walked the length of a landing past a long line of cells. When I came to the end the wardress ordered me into a cell and left me standing in the middle of it. I saw a high barred window with a sloping sill, a bed, a wooden table and a chair. Scanning the room more slowly, I took in the other details: a slop pail, a chamber pot, a washstand with basin and jug; tin plate, tin mug, knife, fork, spoon. Every object was stamped with a dark blue crown.

Somebody had flung a pail of water over the floor, and I could feel the damp seeping through the sole of my shoe. It was icy on my foot. A naked light bulb hung from the ceiling like a miniature moon, and looking at it I had the idea that my life was a window of fixed dimensions, and small things had spread out to fill it. But before I had time to think anything else, the door slammed behind me and the light went out.

Chapter 9

The first night I spent in prison I didn't sleep at all. I kept expecting the door to open and the mistake to be discovered. In my mind it was only a matter of time, and I wanted to be ready when it happened. I also felt too angry to sleep. So I sat fully clothed on the edge of the bed, watching the place on the floor where the shadows of the bars waxed and waned with the moon. Even in the darkest part of the night, my ears could detect the distant clash of metal on metal, as if the day's sounds continued to lap, and every now and then reinforced one another to an audible pitch.

The echo, and the icy draught, were the first things I noticed about being in prison. But there were other things too. For instance, there was no light switch inside my cell, or handle to the door. There was a peephole, but this was for looking in, not out. A thin strip of painted metal hung down from the wall, which I assumed was a bell. But when I pulled it, nothing happened. So I had the feeling that nothing, not even a strip of metal, connected me to the outside world. Of course I understood that that was the punishment, and I was glad when the first ray of sunlight entered my cell, because then my ordeal was over. It was impossible to believe that I would spend another night like that. The tension went out of my limbs, and for the first time I lay back on the bed.

A bit later a loud clanging started up and a wardress unlocked the door. She ordered me out and I joined a long line of women trooping along the landing. Most of them had dark moons under their eyes and a sort of glazed look, as if they were sleepwalking. We reached the centre and from there marched out into a courtyard. At the entrance to the yard a wardress handed us each a few sheets of paper. At the far end was a long row of lavatories in wooden cubicles.

There were too few cubicles for the number of women, so I had to wait my turn. But I soon noticed that one of the cubicles wasn't occupied. The door stood ajar and I made my way towards it. It was clean inside, but there was no lock on the door. When I emerged, a group of women stood staring at me. For a moment nobody spoke. Then one of them asked, 'Didn't you see the sign?' She pointed and I looked behind me. On the door of the cubicle was a large red V. I hadn't noticed it before. My first thought was that it stood for victory. But according to the woman, that cubicle was reserved for women with venereal disease.

A few more women joined the crowd and asked the others what was going on. There was some whispering and they all stared at me. But I couldn't understand what all the fuss was about and I found it funny. I would have laughed but then I remembered I was in prison. A moment later the wardress shouted at us to 'break it up'. Immediately the crowd dispersed and the women fell into line to troop back inside.

For breakfast we were given porridge and strong tea in handleless mugs. Afterwards we returned to our cells. I sat down on the bed and waited for something to happen. I must have waited about half an hour before a wardress appeared in the doorway. I couldn't be sure if she was the one who had unlocked my door earlier, as they all looked alike, and after a day it was only by their footsteps that I could tell them apart. It didn't matter anyway, because I was about to be released and I would probably never set eyes on her again.

I asked her where she was taking me but she didn't reply. She just barked directions and I followed them until I found myself back at the centre. From there we entered a long passage, then another, and another. Finally we mounted a flight of stairs and crossed a landing towards a large wood-panelled door. All the time my shadow kept a constant distance behind me, and I could hear the keys swinging at her waist.

The door was opened by a smart young woman with honey-coloured hair. She wore a brown tweed suit and highly polished brogues. She opened her mouth to say something but then stopped and glanced down at my uniform. She looked surprised. I don't know why, but my heart leapt to see that look and I thought I knew what was going to happen next. She said, 'Hello. I'm Miss Miller,' and stepped back to let me into the room. The wardress stayed outside.

The room was airy and light, with an unobstructed view from the window. From where I stood I could see rooftops, trees and spires, and I had the impression of having risen to the surface and filling my lungs with air. Miss Miller sat down behind a large desk in front of the window and clasped her hands on top of a leather blotter.

The blotter was stamped with a dark blue crown, identical to the one on the chamber pot in my cell. She asked me to sit down and then she explained that she was from the War Office.

Before she could go on I told her there had been some kind of misunderstanding. I was not the person the police were looking for. They had obviously been given the wrong information and I would be grateful if she could set everything straight, because I was a doctor and there were patients waiting to see me. I spoke very calmly and afterwards I folded my hands in my lap and waited for her to apologise. I had already decided that that was the best way to get what I wanted. She looked at me with a quizzical expression, then picked up a sheet of paper from the blotter, read out a name and address, and asked if they were mine. They were. 'In that case,' she said, 'There has been no mistake.'

After that she explained the situation. She spoke in a very businesslike way and I noticed she didn't smile. According to her, new laws had been brought in only two days earlier. They were emergency measures designed especially for wartime. Under the new regulations, people who were suspected of being involved in Fifth Column activities could be arrested and detained. She asked me if I knew what was meant by Fifth Column and I said, 'Yes, you mean spies.' But she shook her head. It wasn't just spying, as the man in the street might understand it. It also meant associating with 'hostile persons'.

She then explained that I was being detained under these laws. So naturally I asked her who were the hostile persons I was supposed to have associated with. She looked at me intently and said, 'Anna Petrova.' After a pause, and still in the same pleasant voice, she asked me, 'You don't deny it then?' I said, 'No,' but in an absent-minded way, because I was thinking about Anna. I hadn't thought about her since the day she was arrested at the bird fair. I had assumed then that she was out of my life; that I would never see or hear from her again. But looking back on it, it was odd that the police had never come to question me about that day, or taken my statement.

I was about to say something when Miss Miller interrupted. It was as if she had read my thoughts. She said, 'Anna Petrova stabbed a man. She was arrested. You haven't seen her since.' She then told me that Anna had been charged with committing a violent assault. But on the same day that the stabbing took place, she had been under observation by another branch of the authorities. That morning she had been followed to the headquarters of a radio station that was suspected of broadcasting enemy propaganda. Now Anna was going to be tried for her part in crimes against the state.

There was a pause before she spoke again. 'I know it's a lot to take in, but have you any questions?' She said it kindly and I found myself liking her, even though she was my captor. And yet it wasn't her fault. She was just following orders. I asked her what all this had to do with me. She said I was known to have been to Anna's restaurant and to have received several visits from her. I pointed out that as far as I knew, going to a restaurant was not illegal, but she didn't reply. So then I asked, 'What is the charge against me?'

She gave me an odd look, as if I was being slow, and all this had been explained. There was no charge, she told me. She hesitated, then in a thoughtful voice she said: 'In a way you've been let off lightly.' According to her, I was lucky that no charges had been made against me. When it was all over I would have no criminal record. It wouldn't affect my life. Instead I was being detained under the new laws, which meant there would be no charges, no trial, and no term set.

I noticed that she was fiddling with a ring on her left hand: pulling it almost off the finger, then pushing it back on. Watching her, it occurred to me that there were certain questions I was supposed to ask. For instance, I wanted to know how long I would be kept there. When I spoke my voice sounded thin and fragile and distant. She said, 'That's a matter for the committee to decide. I just conduct the preliminary interview. Your case will be reviewed in due course.' I thought about that phrase: 'in due course'. She was being evasive and I was annoyed. After all, it was I who had spent the night in a cell. It seemed to me very important to know when I would be freed, so I rephrased my question: 'When will I be released?' She sat back in her chair and stared at the blotter. I realised that she was weighing up possible answers. After a minute she said, 'A month, perhaps longer.'

I looked at her for a long time, trying to organise my thoughts. In my mind nothing had been resolved and I had a feeling that I had forgotten something. Then I remembered what it was I was meant to say. It was the most elementary statement for a person in my predicament, and I couldn't understand why it hadn't occurred to me earlier. But then you always assume the authorities are on your side until they insist they are not. I told her I wanted to see a lawyer.

As soon as I said it her expression altered. I thought she was looking at me with something like pity. Suddenly I had the feeling that a certain combination of words, spoken now, would save me. But the words wouldn't come, and soon it would be too late. My head began to throb. She explained that I wasn't entitled to see a lawyer. The regulations were very clear on that point and besides, I hadn't been accused of any crime. Then, as if to make up for it, she repeated what she had said earlier: 'The committee will review your case in due course.'

There was that phrase again: 'in due course'. I hated it and yet it was meaningless. At the same time it became clear to me that this woman could not help me and I thought about Morris. I told her that I wanted to make a phone call, or send a telegram. 'I'm afraid that's not allowed,' she said, and she sounded genuinely apologetic. She was still tugging at the ring and I realised that somewhere a fiancé was waiting for her. I asked her to send a message for me. But that too was against the regulations. That's when I stopped asking questions. I felt trapped in the same way I had in the bird market, only this time there was no one to lead me out.

By now Miss Miller was skirting the desk. The interview would soon be over but the words that would save me still wouldn't come. She had got as far as the middle of the room when she turned back to me with an exclamation. 'Oh!' she said, 'I forgot. You shouldn't have been given uniform. Detainees are permitted to wear their own clothes.' She apologised for the mistake, but the regulations were new to the prison staff as well and I would just have to bear with them. Then she smiled for the first time, turned round and continued to cross the room. I got up and followed her. At the door she told me that my clothes would be returned to me later that day. It was my last chance but still I couldn't speak. I walked past her and the door closed behind me.

It was dark in the passage but I could see the keys glinting at the wardress's waist. Suddenly, out of nowhere, an image came into my mind of the tall woman with the gold bracelets. I had not seen her since the day before, and I had a sudden, irrational desire to know what had happened to her. But I couldn't remember her name, and almost as soon as the idea came to me I knew it was hopeless, because wherever she was, she was no longer defined by the bracelets.

I don't remember the journey back to my cell, because I kept my eyes on the ground, and all sounds were blocked out by the dull, rhythmic thud of the feet behind me.

Chapter 10

For the first month I was in prison, I existed in a kind of vacuum. I had no idea what was going to happen to me. But I kept remembering Miss Miller's words. According to her, my fate was tied to Anna's. If Anna had done something bad, I would be punished. That didn't seem right or fair. But at the same time I couldn't allow myself to think that I had done nothing wrong, because if there was no reason for my being there, then there was no reason why I should be released. That was the logical conclusion and yet it didn't bear thinking about.

During that time, I ran the whole gamut of emotions. First I was frightened, then angry, then depressed. Through it all one idea stayed with me: that I had somehow become invisible. I heard nothing from Morris, and I didn't allow myself to think about him. But once or twice, in the middle of the night, I woke with the feeling that he had just been there. The smell of his skin filled my nostrils. Then the sensation vanished and I remembered that I was utterly alone.

To begin with, only a few of the cells on my landing were occupied. But they very quickly filled up, and before long the new arrivals were living two to a cell. If I sat on my bed, with my legs crossed and my back against the wall, I could see directly into a woman's cell on the opposite side of the landing. This woman interested me because she was always busy. Her name was April and she looked like a beautiful doll, with bluish-white skin, wide blue eyes and long blonde hair. Sometimes she smiled and waved at me. Other times she moved about, rearranging the furniture, or dusting the surfaces with an old rag, or folding and refolding her few items of clothing.

Once, as I was watching, she carefully removed her shoes, climbed up on the bed and swiped at a cobweb in the corner of the ceiling with an unravelled stocking. She must have missed, because from then on I often used to catch her standing perfectly still in the middle of the cell, staring up at that same spot on the ceiling. For a long time I didn't speak to her. The other women said she was mad, but I envied her. At least she had found a way to distract herself. Then one day she came up to me in the queue for the kitchen.

As detainees we were allowed to cook our own food. It was one of our privileges. We bought it with coupons in the prison shop, and cooked it over a gas ring in an alcove at the end of the landing. But with only one ring for fifty women there was always a queue. I was waiting my turn to warm some milk, when April stepped up and asked if she could go ahead of me. She explained that she was in a hurry and so I agreed. It made no difference to me. The other women gave her resentful looks and muttered things I couldn't hear, but she didn't seem to notice.

Later that day I was lying on my bed when I saw that her cell was empty. After a moment she appeared in my doorway. But she didn't say anything. She just stood there, looking at me. Then she came closer and bent forward, bringing her face quite close to mine, and it occurred to me that she was short-sighted. She said, 'Are you spying on me?' I was surprised, but she seemed more curious than hostile and I said, 'No.' She sat down on the bed and started to pull at a piece of hair, twisting it into a stiff rod but never taking her eyes off me. There was a pause and then she smiled and said, 'I believe you.'

She had been meaning to talk to me for some time, she said. She'd written a poem for me but it was only in her head because 'they' wouldn't allow her paper or pencils. In this poem, I was a duchess who had murdered her husband in a jealous rage, so I had to be put away. She had to be careful, though, because it was her poems that had got her into trouble in the first place. They thought she was sending coded messages in the form of rhymes, and the extraordinary thing was, they were right. 'I was doing it and I didn't even know it. The idea would just pop into my head and I would write it down.'

She had to be protected from herself and that's why she was here. But she was quite glad about it, because it meant she couldn't do any harm. Besides, there was plenty to be getting on with. Just keeping her cell clean and tidy was a full-time job. If she stayed away for too long the dust got out of hand. You had to keep on top of it. At that she jumped up and said she had to be going. She had just wanted to tell me about the poem. She seemed to be waiting for something so I thanked her and she left. But it was then that I thought she would make a good case study. If I recorded my observations of her it would be a way of passing the time.

About a week later a wardress came to my cell and told me to accompany her. Any break from the routine was welcome, even if you didn't know what it entailed, and I was grateful. I quickly realised that we were heading towards the outside and I felt a great surge of joy. But I didn't say anything, because I had already learnt that there was no point. The wardress wouldn't reply.

In the reception area I waited while she spoke to another wardress. They both came towards me and I was told that I was to be seen by the committee. A moment later I was walking through the prison gate, with the sunshine on my neck and a grey guardian on either side of me. I could hardly believe it, because I was walking down a street, and people who were free were passing within a few yards of me. To my surprise, the wardresses didn't handcuff me. My first impulse was to make a dash for it. It even occurred to me that they had left the handcuffs off on purpose, to give me a chance to escape. But what if I was about to be released? In the end I wanted to hear what the committee had to say.

As I walked I looked about me. There were the sandbags, and above me the swarm of barrage balloons, and then turning a corner I came face to face with a broad slot of sky. Either side of it stood two houses, perfectly intact, but of the house between them there was nothing left: only a pile of rubble with a couple of firemen picking their way over it, and smoke rising up in places. I stopped to look, but the wardresses immediately shouted at me to keep walking. When I asked them what had happened they told me a bomb had fallen in the night. A family had died.

From then I paid more attention to the passers-by, and I noticed that they were acting strangely. There was a sort of wariness about them and one man even crossed the road to get out of my path. I could understand why, and I didn't blame him. He thought I was a criminal. But there was one old woman who behaved differently. Perhaps she noticed that I wasn't wearing uniform, that I was a different kind of prisoner. She stopped when we were still some way off, and leaning on her walking stick, removed a large white handkerchief from a pocket in her skirt. Then she fixed her bloodshot eyes on me and slowly wiped her mouth. For a moment I thought she was going to spit on me. But she just tucked the handkerchief back in her pocket and gave me a polite nod.

The committee sat in a disused hotel not far from the prison. The two wardresses marched me into a large room and left me standing in the middle of a vast expanse of parquet. It must have been a ballroom once. Huge gilt mirrors hung on the walls and glass chandeliers hung down from the ceiling. At the far end, facing me, three men sat behind a long trestle table covered in green baize, their backs to two large bay windows. To one side sat a young woman with her legs crossed and a notepad open on her knee. It was Miss Miller.

After clearing his throat the man in the middle introduced himself. He was the chairman of the committee and it was his job to determine whether or not my detention should continue. There was an echo in the room and he spoke very precisely. With the light behind him his face was obscured, but I could tell that he wore a pince-nez and some kind of lotion in his hair, because both reflected the light. He was also a good head shorter than either of his colleagues, and he wore a stiff white collar. At his right hand stood a pile of documents almost a foot high. The two men either side of him were busy shuffling papers and occasionally sliding them across to him.

The chairman proceeded to interrogate me. But first he pointed out that it was in my interests to give as full and frank an account of myself as possible. I didn't mind: the sooner he obtained the facts, the sooner I would be released. But I quickly realised that certain facts held more importance for him than others. For instance, he was very interested in the nature of my relationship with Anna. I described our first meeting, on the day of the riot, and my later visit to the restaurant. But before I could say anything else he pounced forward, so that his pince-nez glinted in the light from the window. 'We know all about your little midnight escapade,' he said in a sneering tone, and then he asked me if I was going to deny that I had helped Anna to post her stickers.

I was surprised by the attack but also a little indignant. On the contrary, I told him, I had no intention of denying it. He asked me if I agreed with the sentiment, that war destroyed workers, and I replied, without hesitating, 'Yes.' I was about to add that it was obviously true, but I stopped myself. I realised it would be better not to irritate him. Instead I explained that I had never considered the posting of the stickers a very significant event. In fact, it was almost certainly a waste of time, as people pay very little attention to walls.

At that the chairman removed his pince-nez and looked sharply sideways at Miss Miller, asking her to take a note. He dictated: 'Prisoner defiant. Regrets only that her actions did not succeed.' But that wasn't what I had meant. I opened my mouth to protest, but the chairman interrupted. 'Please speak only when you are spoken to,' he snapped. Miss Miller bent over her pad, and for a few moments he and his colleagues conferred in low murmurs. Then their heads separated and the chairman began to speak in a rapid, staccato voice.

In two days time, he announced, the trial of Anna Petrova would begin. She stood accused of serious crimes against the state, namely the broadcasting of subversive propaganda. Under interrogation she had admitted that I had collaborated with her in an earlier campaign. I was also known to have visited the headquarters of the radio station on at least one occasion. 'That makes you a prime suspect,' he said. 'You will remain in detention pending the outcome of the trial.'

He carried on talking, but I stopped listening, because in my mind something had slotted into place. Suddenly I saw myself through his eyes. I was no longer a woman standing alone in an empty ballroom. I stood at the head of a crowd, and behind me stretched an invisible army of traitors. It was an incredible idea, and yet it made sense of everything that had happened.

When he had finished speaking he asked me if I had anything to say. This time the words came easily. I told him, 'You think I'm a traitor. But all I did was post some stickers. I didn't force anybody to read them.' Even as I said it I realised that I was in the wrong, because under the new regulations the posting of stickers was outlawed. So in fact there had been no mistake after all. I was a criminal, and it was right that I should be detained, even though the regulations hadn't existed when I broke them.

All this came to me in a flash. Slowly I became aware

that Miss Miller had put down her pen and was looking at me. It was a sad look and I had a feeling that at last she understood my position: that for me there was no way out. But it was only a feeling. There was silence in the room and then the chairman asked me, 'Do you understand what you have been told?' He leaned forward expectantly, placing his elbows on the table and removing his pince-nez. Suddenly the sight of him filled me with anger: that this man who knew nothing about me could decide my fate. My heart beat faster and my hands shook. I told him that I had done nothing wrong; that he couldn't keep me like this. But even as I said it I remembered where I had heard those words before, and I knew that it was hopeless.

When he spoke again it was like the voice of death. The words boomed out at me from the dark oval of his face. He said, 'You are a menace to society. Society must be protected from you and you must be protected from yourself.' Then he explained that I was not a criminal in the eyes of the law, and my imprisonment was in no way a punishment. I was merely being prevented from committing acts that might threaten the security of the nation. For the time being he did not feel able to approve my release. But my case would be reviewed again in due course. With that he brought a stamp down noisily on the file that lay open in front of him and put it to one side.

I left the room in a sort of trance, accompanied by the two wardresses, who had been standing by the door all the time. There was a pain in my stomach and I was only dimly aware of a woman sitting on a bench against the wall of the corridor. There were other figures present too but I paid no attention to them. I was thinking about what the chairman had said. If I understood him correctly, I was paying for a crime I might commit in the future. There was no possible defence, because how could I deny something that had not yet happened? As I passed her the woman on the bench leaned forward and spoke to me. A moment later I felt a tug on my sleeve. She was trailing me, trying to get my attention. I didn't stop, though, or look back, and it was only when I got out into the street that I realised who she was.

When I reached my cell, I lay down on the bed and closed my eyes. A terrible fatigue had come over me, and all I wanted to do was sleep. But I couldn't. My mind was racing, and I had to be careful not to sink into despair. There was one idea that kept straying into my thoughts: that I might never walk down the street or look out over the river or talk to Morris again. That I might be locked up indefinitely.

When I opened my eyes, April was standing about three feet away from me. She was frowning and biting at the skin around her thumbnail. She took a step forward and asked me why I had ignored her in the hotel. She seemed agitated. I told that I had had some bad news and I wasn't thinking straight. The committee had decided not to release me.

Her eyes widened and she said, 'Is that all?' I looked at her and she went on. She had been worried that I'd told them about her poem. Somehow they had found out that she had been writing more poetry and had decided not to let her go. But it didn't really matter, she said. They were wise men and they knew her almost better than she knew herself. They knew she couldn't always be held responsible for her actions. She accepted their decision, and she was glad, because after all this time she wouldn't feel safe on the outside. 'This is my home now,' she said.

She laughed, and I turned towards the wall. Something very bad must have happened to her, I thought, to make her want to stay in this place. But however hard I tried, I couldn't imagine a thing that bad. To my mind, a sane person was one who would rather be anywhere else than in gaol. I felt sorry for her, but at the same time frightened, because what if she had found the best solution?

I was just thinking this when a wardress walked past the doorway shouting. It was five minutes until lights out, and all women had to get back to their cells. April leaned over me and her breath warmed my cheek. She said, 'Don't worry, you're quite safe here.' Then the door slammed and the light went out. I closed my eyes and tried to sleep. But as soon as the wardress's footsteps had receded the night sounds started up, and I lay awake listening to them.

Chapter 11

One day, the fat wardress with the lopsided face waddled into my cell and told me there was someone to see me. A number of us prisoners filed through a door into a long, low room. At the far end the visitors filed in through another door. Beyond theirs I could see the sky: a rectangle of brilliant white. There were no windows but I could tell from their clothes that it was summer.

The room was filled with small wooden tables closely packed in rows. The visitors took one side and the inmates the other, so that I was facing the door to the outside. I sat down and looked around me. A tall, skinny man with a moustache was making his way to the table next to mine. He was smiling but the fat woman sitting at it hadn't yet noticed him. A moment later, she burst into tears. She stood up and started to move round the table with her arms outstretched. But a wardress ordered her to sit down again. No touching allowed. The man sat down and leant forward to speak to her. She was sobbing noisily and he was trying to soothe her. But her hand kept reaching out for his, and each time it did he glanced nervously at the wardress and pulled his own away.

Just then I spotted Morris. He was wearing a soldier's uniform: khaki trousers and a khaki jacket gathered in at the waist. The trousers tapered into a pair of bicycle clips that he had forgotten to remove. His hair had been cut short, which made him look gaunt, and distorted his features. He came through the door and stopped. A wardress standing behind a little desk called him over and pointed to the string bag he was carrying. She put her nose inside and checked the contents, then nodded and handed it back.

Morris and I looked at each other for a long time. I would have liked to touch him and I understood how the fat woman felt. He said, 'They're treating you all right?' and I nodded, even though it was a pointless question. Then he picked up the string bag from the floor and placed it on the table. 'I've brought you a few things.' I looked in the bag. There was a newspaper, some picture postcards, a bottle of stout and a little parcel of granulated sugar. He had obviously been saving up his rations. I thanked him and asked if next time he would bring soap. He looked puzzled and I explained: the worst thing about prison was the terrible grime. Somehow you had to stop it seeping into you.

The fat woman's sobs were getting louder and Morris had to raise his voice to make himself heard. He'd been trying to get to see me for months, he said, but they wouldn't let him. So he'd had to tell them I was his fiancée. At first they didn't believe it but then, out of the blue, they changed their minds. He stopped talking and we looked at each other again. After a while I asked him, 'You're a soldier then?' He blushed and looked down at his uniform. He'd thought about it long and hard, he said. But in the end it was his duty and he couldn't shirk it. He was living at the barracks and it wasn't such a bad life. But he missed his old job and his boss had been sorry to see him go.

He lit a cigarette. I asked him about the surgery and he said it was still standing. But the docks had been almost completely destroyed and when an oil tanker was hit it had taken them a week to put out the flames. The heat had blistered the paint on the houses for miles around. The warehouse where the boxing match had taken place had scored a direct hit and there was nothing left of the jetty. 'I went to look for it last week. All that's left is a pile of rubble and a few burnt planks. The rest fell into the river.' Most of the shops in the main road were still there, except for the chicken shop. Klamm had a nasty shock waiting for him when he came back, he said. But that wouldn't be for a while yet. According to Samuel, he had been sent to a camp.

I tried to picture the jetty, and Klamm's shop, and the memory of them filled me with a kind of fear. Those places I remembered no longer existed. The world I knew was changing beyond all recognition. Even Morris looked different. I couldn't imagine standing naked in front of him any more. Then again, perhaps it was I who had changed. There were no mirrors in the prison and I hadn't looked at myself in months.

He asked me when they were going to set me free but I didn't know. He looked at me with an odd expression and then he smiled. That was a good sign, he said. They'd be sure to let me know if it was going to be a long stretch. Otherwise where would be the punishment? I didn't say anything. He was only trying to be kind, and yet I think he was wrong. And after all, it was enough for me to have him there. He didn't have to speak. Beneath the table I felt his leg press against mine. I returned the pressure, and the rough material pricked my skin. 'Just remember,' he said, still smiling. 'You're my fiancée now.'

The wardress on duty shouted 'Two minutes!' and the fat woman gave a loud yelp. Morris and I turned to look at her. Raising her behind off the seat she stretched forward to grasp the man by the arms. 'Do something!' she shouted at him, 'You've got to do something!' All around us the conversations stopped and people turned to stare, but she seemed oblivious. The man's moustache twitched and he caught my eye. But she had him pinioned to the seat and he was helpless. He tried to say something but she kept on shouting hysterically, 'Get me out of here! Get me out of here!'

Suddenly the wardress was dragging her off him and telling her to pull herself together, or there would be no more visits. The woman replied that it didn't matter to her. 'I can't stand the sight of him,' she said. The man and the woman looked at each other in silence, and then in a quiet voice she said, 'I'd like to go back to my cell now.' After the wardress had led her away, the man looked around hurriedly as if he had lost something, then picked up his hat and left. Visiting time was over and Morris got to his feet. But just before he left he told me he'd be back next week.

When I got to my cell I lay down and thought about Morris. I was wondering how I would feel if he were killed in action. At first I would be overwhelmed by grief. I would miss talking to him and laughing at his jokes. More than that I would miss lying beside him, naked, and the smell of his skin. For some reason I found that smell quite addictive. But like most physical addictions it would wear off if unfed and I would get on with my life. You got used to most things after a while. That to me was the saddest part.

I pulled the newspaper out of the bag and unfolded it on the mattress in front of me. I flicked past all the news of the latest military advances, and deaths and casualties, and torpedoed ships, because none of it had anything to do with me. As far as I was concerned, it was taking place in another world. But eventually I came to a small story about accidents in the home. According to a survey, up to eight thousand deaths a year resulted from 'trivial mishaps', such as tripping over torn linoleum, or being scalded by overturned kettles. A spokesman for the Women's Electrical Association said that it was mainly due to badly lit housing. A great deal of research had been carried out in recent years for war purposes, and after the war this would be switched over to improve social conditions. Thanks to the war, thousands of lives might be saved.

I was about to close the newspaper when I noticed a picture on the opposite page. It was of two women standing side by side, holding a shell necklace between them. One was shielding her eyes from the sun and smiling. The other gazed into the camera with a quizzical look. She had beetle-black eyebrows and I recognised the woman with the gold bracelets. Beneath the picture was the caption: 'Mrs Ena Roschowski displays her handiwork.'

At first I was confused. I thought it must be a different woman. But then I realised what had happened. She had been transferred from the prison almost as soon as she had arrived. That happened to a lot of the women. The story described the visit of a government inspector to one of the island camps. There had been reports of a number of suicides. But according to him, most of the women had adapted well. There was a good atmosphere and they had found all sorts of useful pastimes, such as playing bowls on the beach and organising bridge classes. Some had even found a way of earning a few extra pennies by making necklaces out of seashells and selling them to the local townsfolk. The unfortunate death of Mrs Roschowski, whose body had been found washed up on the beach, was a 'unique and regrettable accident'.

Morris didn't come back the next week but the week after. That was as often as we were allowed visitors. As soon as he left I would look forward to the next visit, and when it came it was difficult to believe that two weeks had passed since the last. Sometimes he didn't come at all, for weeks on end, and then I would know that he had been posted overseas, and I would have to wait until his next leave. Occasionally he would send a letter. The days went by in the same monotonous routine, and the only other distraction was my interrogations by the committee. I began to look forward to those too, even though the outcome was always the same. At least it meant a walk through the streets, and a glimpse of people with busy lives.

Once, on my return, I noticed that the other women kept looking at me in a suspicious way. It wasn't just me. Anyone who had recently been before the committee got the same treatment. When I asked April if she'd noticed she laughed and said it was obvious. 'Everyone thinks they are innocent, so someone else must be guilty.

But who? They've no way of telling.' Thinking about it, I understood that she was right. Sometimes April saw things as they were. But as time went by the suspicious glances faded, and people came and went unnoticed. Then I realised that another idea had taken hold: either we were all guilty, or none of us were.

From then on, it was quite common to wake to the sound of a woman losing her mind. The wardresses referred to it as a 'nerve storm'. One morning, for instance, I was woken by muffled cries and the thud and crash of hard surfaces colliding. It happened just before dawn, in the darkest part of the night, and for a moment I was confused, because the sounds were all around me and in the darkness it seemed as if the walls of my cell were under attack. But then I heard a key turning in a lock. A second later, a scream rang out across the landing, and I realised it was one of the women smashing up her cell. Or rather, rearranging it, since every object at her disposal was blunt and indestructible.

I strained my ears to try and locate the commotion, and thereby identify the woman. But it was no good. The wailing had a strange, unearthly quality about it, as of an animal trapped, or a baby in distress, and the auditorium of the prison magnified and displaced it. The woman hardly paused for breath, and I could tell she was turning circles round her cell, because the pitch wavered like the siren on a moving ambulance. After a while the screams subsided, and the landing was quiet again. I couldn't get back to sleep, though, because I kept imagining her being wrestled to the floor by the women in grey, and led away to the padded cells.

That afternoon, I was taken to the hotel. As soon as we had left the prison grounds the two wardresses struck up a conversation. One of them happened to mention the date. I was shocked when I heard it, because over a year had passed since my arrest. It was a beautiful day in late spring, the time of year I liked best, and the sun was warm on my face. I tried to walk as slowly as possible without annoying the wardresses, but still we reached the hotel too soon. A queue of women sat on the bench outside the ballroom and I had to wait my turn. When I entered, the three men took no notice of me. They had their heads together and they were murmuring in low voices. So I amused myself by looking around.

The thing that immediately caught my attention was the pile of documents at the chairman's right hand. Since my last visit it had almost doubled in height. As for the chairman himself, his tie was slightly askew and wisps of hair stood up from his head. I almost felt sorry for him, because it was clear that he had more work than he could manage. But then I realised that this was inevitable. He wasn't dealing with criminals, but with people who might commit a crime, one day. And, well, naturally the latter outnumber the former.

The chairman looked up and cleared his throat. His expression was serious. Skipping the usual preliminaries he said, 'It is my duty to inform you that you are no longer under detention.' Before I could take this in he went on. More evidence had come to light regarding my attempts to undermine the state, he said. As a result charges had been brought against me. My case would now be dealt with in a court of law and I would be entitled to instruct lawyers to act on my behalf.

A few minutes later I was standing outside in the sunshine again, wondering what it all meant. My situation had changed in some important way, but whether for better or worse I couldn't say. I was curious to see what would happen next.

We didn't set off for the prison as usual. The wardresses seemed to be waiting for something and soon enough a car turned into the street. It came to a halt and I was bundled into it. After a short while it drew up outside a police station and I was led into a room full of official-looking people. It was hard to believe that they were all there because of me. A man in a black suit read out the charges against me. He accused me of being a traitor. But according to the wardresses it was just a formality and afterwards I was taken back to the prison and told to pack up my things. One of the wardresses waited to take me to the remand wing, and I was ordered not to speak to the other women. Yet somehow I think they knew what was going on. April stood watching me from the door of her cell and even though I couldn't see the others I felt their eyes boring into me.

The wardress followed me along the landing and when I reached the end I turned to look back. But there was no sign of April and the door to her cell was closed. I was surprised, because our doors were never closed except at night and I felt she was reproaching me in some way. A number of the other women had come out of their cells and were leaning against the wall, their faces turned towards me. One or two were smoking, others dragged their feet in slippers. All wore blank expressions and nobody spoke.

Looking at those women it occurred to me that I no longer had anything in common with them. Some might say I was worse off and yet I think they envied me. There was an event ahead of me that would mark the end of this period of my life, whereas their imprisonment stretched away from them interminably. I was going to stand trial. The crime of which I had been accused was punishable by death, but I was innocent. The prospect of my future filled me with an inexpressible relief. Something had been stripped away from me and I could breathe again.

Chapter 12

As soon as I arrived on the remand wing my life changed completely. For one thing I often got into fights. The other women jostled me in the corridors, and sometimes, when the wardresses weren't looking, I would find myself cornered by five or six of them. On those occasions I had no choice but to defend myself. At first I couldn't understand why they hated me so much, but then I realised: they saw me as a traitor. And yet some of them were murderers. In their eyes my crime was worse than killing. I didn't care though, because now there would have to be a trial, and at the trial I would be found innocent and set free.

Another thing was the women themselves. They didn't have the glazed look of sleepwalkers that I had got used to seeing among the detainees. I think it was because they knew what was going to happen to them. Whether they were guilty or innocent, they would have a chance to put their case.

And then I had frequent visits from my lawyers. There were three of them altogether: one solicitor and two barristers. The solicitor came most often. His name was Crawford and he had a face like a walnut. He smoked French cigarettes, and when he laughed it sounded like someone raking coals. The fingers of his left hand were stained yellow with nicotine. He was always cheerful and as the weeks went by he developed a habit of referring to 'us' and 'we' rather than 'you'. For instance, he might say, 'The evidence against us is purely circumstantial,' as if he and I and the two barristers were all going to be standing in the dock together.

I was flattered. I thought he understood the injustice of my predicament. But at the same time I couldn't help feeling that there was something odd about it. One day, he arrived with the news that the trial date had been set for May, almost two years after my arrest. It seemed like a momentous occasion, and I took the opportunity to enquire why he had never asked if I was guilty. To my surprise he laughed and said, 'Ours is not to reason why.' I realised then that he didn't understand at all. He was only doing his job, and like Miss Miller and the wardresses, he was following orders.

On the morning of the first day of my trial, I walked past the wooden reception cubicles and out into the entrance courtyard. It was drizzling and I noticed that since my first day at the prison someone had planted the flowerbeds. There were a couple of straggling roses, some shrubs not yet in flower, and a great many weeds.

The driver of the van started up the engine, I climbed in beside a wardress and the gates swung open in front of me. As on previous occasions when I had left the prison grounds I felt a great surge of happiness, and yet it was only the dirty grey city streets I was looking at. As we drove through them, I saw that many of the buildings were in ruins, and it occurred to me that people had died. I was more interested in the living, though, and I paid close attention to the pedestrians on the pavement. There was a boy in shorts who was smoking a cigarette as he walked. He must have been about twelve. He had a gas mask slung over his shoulder and a spare cigarette tucked behind his ear. As I watched, he removed the cigarette, lit it from the one in his mouth, then threw the butt into the gutter and continued smoking. There was a jaunty air about him and I could tell he was far from home.

The van came to a halt at a junction and beside it a man emerged from a doorway onto the pavement. He walked a few feet, then stopped and twisted round, tipping his head back. A woman in a dressing gown was leaning out of a first floor window. Her dark hair was tousled and she was waving a silver flask. From the way she was swaying I guessed she was drunk, and for some reason I thought it was Anna. My heart contracted and I caught my breath. But almost as soon as the thought had occurred to me I knew it was impossible. As I watched, the woman blew a kiss to the man below. He looked round in embarrassment, then turned back to her and hurriedly blew one back. A moment later he disappeared round the corner.

At the courthouse the van entered a yard and a portcullis rattled down behind it. I was led into a cell and told to wait. On the wall was a framed picture of the Sword of Justice. The wardress stayed in the room with me. Some time later a policeman opened the door and told us it was time to go. He led me up a staircase and through a doorway, and suddenly, without warning, I found myself in the dock, overlooking the courtroom.

There were a lot of people present and I didn't know any of them. But then I looked down and recognised

Crawford in a smart pinstriped suit. He smiled up at me but I did not smile back, as I was aware of several pairs of eyes watching me. To my left sat the jury. Five of the twelve seats were empty, and at first I was alarmed, thinking I wasn't going to get a fair trial. But then I realised that seven were just as likely to come to the right conclusion as twelve, and that after all this was wartime, and there were certain things one had to do without.

The seven jurors gazed at me intently, and two women in the back row started whispering. Directly in front of them sat an old man. He wore a crumpled jacket over a pullover, and a collar and tie. Where the collar of his shirt rubbed his neck the material was frayed and yellow. As I watched he removed his spectacles, polished them on the hem of his pullover and replaced them on his nose, all without taking his eyes off me. I had the feeling that he was sizing me up and forming an opinion. The idea occurred to me that although the trial hadn't begun yet the outcome had already been decided. In that sense there were things going on in this courtroom that had nothing to do with me.

I couldn't look at the jury after that so I turned away. Opposite me was a raised bench, carved in oak, with three empty chairs set forward. Above me and to my right was the public gallery, empty apart from a single fly growling in the shadows. The press box was empty too, but I wasn't surprised, because Crawford had explained all this beforehand. He had said that the sensitive nature of the charges against me meant that the trial was to be held in camera.

Looking down I saw the rolled wigs of the lawyers,

who were busily conferring or sifting through documents, and behind them, in a corner, the stenographer. Her hands rested in her lap and she stared unseeingly into space. I realised she was bored, and I felt the urge to shake her, because what was about to take place could decide the rest of my life. But of course it was quite natural, and I couldn't blame her. It was just another day at the office for her.

There were three sharp knocks and a hush fell over the room. The usher leapt to his feet and said, 'Be upstanding in court!' A number of people filed through a door at the end of the bench opposite, with the judge bringing up the rear. He wore scarlet robes and carried a folded piece of black cloth and a pair of white gloves. He was very old and his shoulders were hunched so that they rose higher than the top of his wig. He sat in the middle of the three chairs, directly opposite me, and yet I noticed he didn't look at me. The clerk read out the charges and asked me what I pleaded. I said, 'Not guilty.' As I did so I felt the jurors' eyes swivel towards me.

The jury was sworn in and the prosecuting lawyer got to his feet, cleared his throat and addressed them. He explained that he was going to prove 'beyond a reasonable doubt' that I had formed a small but essential link in an ignominious chain of treachery. He said that my actions alone had placed the entire national war effort in jeopardy, but that my crime had to be viewed in the light of a wider conspiracy, a highly organised network of spies whose ultimate goal was to see this country 'brought to her knees'. If the jury wanted an indication of the seriousness of my crime, they need look no further than the fact that the trial had to be conducted in camera, and that they themselves were sworn to secrecy.

As he spoke the prosecutor threw me hostile glances and jabbed his fat forefinger at me. Once he even turned to face me fully, while still addressing the jury, and I saw that he was a drinker. Tiny red capillaries crisscrossed his nose and cheeks, and his eyes were a pale and watery blue. In a passionate speech he explained to the jury that when one country was planning to invade another, the first step was to gauge the mood of that country, so that the attack could be timed for when morale was at its lowest, and its defences most vulnerable. According to him, our enemies were doing just this. They were searching for a weak point. And as a doctor, I was perfectly placed to find it. Simply by passing on what I saw and heard from my patients, I was providing the enemy with a weapon that would make it invincible.

The prosecutor wandered over to the jury box and rested his large hands on the wooden rail, leaning forward so that he cast a shadow over the old man, who had to look up to see his face. He was coming to the end of his speech, and asking the jury to consider the potential consequences of my actions, had I not been caught. 'Millions of lives might have been lost, ladies and gentlemen of the jury. Innocent lives. Ordinary people like you and I. I ask you, when considering the evidence put before you, to keep that fact in mind.'

The prosecutor returned to his seat and drank from a glass of water. Looking down at him I was filled with admiration. His speech had gone on for a very long time and by subtle degrees he had managed to transform me from a nobody into a person with the power to determine the outcome of the war. I had never thought of myself as a gatherer of information, but of course, in a way, I was. Anyway, the old man's eyes bored into me and I realised that that was what he saw.

The judge mumbled something and then raised his voice and announced that the court would be adjourned until the afternoon. Then he rose, gripping the silk trim of his robe with one arthritic hand. The usher asked the court to be upstanding, and he hobbled out. I was taken back down to the cells where a policeman asked me if I wanted something to eat. I said no, because although I had been hungry earlier, I had lost my appetite. But he brought a tray anyway, with some kind of stew and potato, and dumped it on a table in the corner.

In the afternoon it was the turn of the more senior of my two barristers to address the jury. Pacing up and down slowly in front of them, and turning his head to make eye contact with each one in turn, he told them that they would hear a lot of emotional talk during the coming days. That was only natural in wartime, he said, when the defendant stood accused of crimes amounting to treason. 'But,' he added, raising a finger in the air, 'I beg you to look past the words, and to make your judgement on the facts alone. If you do, you will see that the evidence is purely circumstantial.'

The first witness for the prosecution was Miss Miller, the young woman from the War Office. She wore a black hat tilted over her forehead and gloves. She stepped up to the rail without a glance in my direction, and the prosecutor held up a thick wedge of papers and asked that these, the transcripts of my interviews before the committee, be recorded as evidence. She was asked when Anna and I first met, to which she replied that it was during the riot. Anna had been marching with the blackshirts when she was injured by a piece of flying debris. I had tended the wound.

The prosecutor asked her for a date. He wanted to get the chronology exactly right, he said. Then he asked her how much time had elapsed between that first meeting and the midnight expedition to post the stickers. A month, she replied. Turning toward the jury the prosecutor said that it was well known that the blackshirts were opposed to the war; that they favoured some kind of peaceful alliance with the enemy. At least that was his understanding and he asked Miss Miller to confirm it. 'That's correct,' she agreed.

And yet, the prosecutor went on, soon after meeting me, Anna had decided that the blackshirts' ideas weren't radical enough for her. She opted instead to 'go it alone'. Was that, in Miss Miller's opinion, a coincidence? Almost immediately, as if she had been expecting the question, she answered, 'No.' The prosecutor wanted to know if she had any evidence to support her conjecture. Glancing at the judge, and then back to the prosecutor, she said that when I had been asked about the posters, I had described them as a waste of time. Those were the exact words I had used.

At this point the judge intervened. He asked Miss Miller if she was suggesting that I had influenced Anna, that I had 'egged her on'. That was the committee's conclusion, she replied. He then wanted to know what my attitude had been during the interrogations. Looking down, Miss Miller frowned at her gloved hands. I had certainly answered all the questions put to me, she said. But there was something odd about my behaviour. 'It was as if she couldn't understand what all the fuss was about,' she said, 'as if what she had done was the most natural thing in the world.'

The judge thanked her and the prosecutor said he had no more questions. Then my lawyer rose and arranged his robes around him. He smiled at the young woman and joked that he was a bit slower than his learned colleague. But he too wanted to get the chronology right, starting with the day on which Anna Petrova was arrested for committing a violent assault. On that day I was alleged to have accompanied her to the headquarters of the radio station. And yet I was on the premises less than ten minutes. There had been no sightings of me at that address either before or since.

In a sneering voice he asked her, 'Would you have the court believe that a woman who had spent no more than ten minutes in the company of these traitors was actually the brains behind the operation?' Again Miss Miller seemed prepared. She smiled and said it was a simple ploy to detract suspicion from me, the ringleader. From the beginning I had controlled the operation from afar. My lawyer pointed out that in fact there was no evidence that I had communicated with anyone at the aforementioned address, either by letter or telephone or in person. In the same sneering voice he added, 'Unless you consider telepathy to be a reliable means of communication?'

A murmur of laughter went round the courtroom and Miss Miller blushed. Before she could speak, my lawyer tucked his thumbs into the lapels of his robe and went on. 'I put it to you,' he said in a booming voice, 'That my client knew nothing of these shady goings on. That in fact she was just an innocent bystander, and that the Petrova woman and her lover Nolan hatched the whole plot between them. Furthermore, I put it to you that my client has already paid dearly for a crime which she did not commit.'

Miss Miller shifted her feet uncomfortably and looked down at the prosecuting lawyer as if to ask for help. She started to say something about 'necessary measures' but my lawyer interrupted. 'Please just answer yes or no. Is it conceivable that the accused knew nothing of this affair?'

Miss Miller glared at the prosecutor. Then, in a quiet voice, she admitted that it was possible. With a swish of his gown my lawyer then turned to the judge to announce that he had no further questions and sat down. The young woman seemed reluctant to leave the witness box, and before she did so, threw me a reproachful glance. I hardly noticed it though, because I was in a bit of a daze. It was as if I was watching a tug of war, only I was the one being pulled in opposite directions. I hardly knew whether I was guilty or innocent.

When the prosecutor called out the name of the next witness there was a commotion among my lawyers, and the more senior of them jumped to his feet. 'Objection, Your Honour!' he said, 'The defence has no knowledge of this witness!' Calmly the prosecutor turned to the judge and explained that some last minute evidence had come to light. The judge asked them both to approach the bench and some conferring went on. A few minutes later the witness was called again and the balding detective appeared in the witness box. He wore a plain double-breasted suit and clutched his hat in his hand. He looked at me and then he turned to the judge with an ingratiating smile.

In answer to a question from the prosecutor he confirmed that he was a detective and that on a certain date he and a junior colleague had visited my place of residence in connection with 'an incident'. He was asked to give details and he mentioned the officer who died on the day of the riot. The man they had wanted to question was called Janowitz. He was thought to have been on the barricade that day.

'Is this the same Janowitz who lives in the flat beneath the accused?' asked the prosecutor in an offhand way. Yes, he replied, only when he and a colleague arrived at the surgery I had informed them that Janowitz couldn't possibly have been on the barricade as he had been with me.

My lawyer leapt to his feet and protested. He couldn't see the relevance of this line of questioning. But the prosecutor insisted that he was about to establish its relevance. My lawyer sat down, looking unhappy, and the prosecutor asked the detective to go on. The detective cleared his throat. 'The doctor informed us that Mr Janowitz had come across an injured boy and brought him to the surgery for assistance. She later gave a statement to the same effect. But the boy's version of events differed in a number of crucial respects.' Janowitz was arrested and taken in for questioning. The prosecutor asked if any charges were brought and the detective said, 'No.' Another suspect had come forward and Janowitz was later released. But that false information had hampered the investigation and set it back by months.

The prosecutor then wanted to know if the person who had provided the false information was present. I thought it a pointless question, since it was obviously me he was referring to, but he explained that it was 'for the benefit of the court'. The detective looked towards me and nodded. 'That's her,' he said. A rustle went through the room and the prosecutor whirled round to face the stenographer. Triumphantly he asked her to note that the witness had indicated the defendant. He then turned to the jury, telling them that this was yet another example of how I had attempted to undermine the state. According to him, it clearly showed my utter contempt for law and order.

He sat down and my lawyer rose half way out of his seat to say that he had no questions for the witness. The court was adjourned for the day and the judge left. But outside in the corridor Crawford marched straight up to me and demanded to know why I hadn't told him about the episode with the policeman. I said I had completely forgotten about it. It was just something I had done on the spur of the moment and I didn't see what it had to do with my case. He looked at me in astonishment and said, 'Don't you realise that everything is relevant to your case?'

I thought for a moment, and it occurred to me that he

was right. When you are living your life, you judge each situation on its merits and act accordingly. But when you are accused of a crime, every action suddenly points to your guilt or innocence. All your actions flow together with a single theme. It was a remarkable idea, and yet in many ways entirely sensible.

Returning to the prison I noticed that it had been raining. The van splashed through puddles on the road and there was a smell of wet tarmac. A couple of old men in macintoshes carried furled umbrellas under one arm and the evening paper under the other. I thought of them hurrying home to their wives for supper and I envied them. I was tired and my back ached from having stood for so long.

In my cell I went straight to sleep and dreamed I was sitting in an old oak tree. I was high above the ground and beneath me the trunk stretched away, perfectly smooth and without branches. I couldn't remember how I had got there, and I wasn't sure how I would get down. But for a moment I was happy to be sitting in that place, with the canopy rustling around me and a breeze stroking my calves.

Chapter 13

Morris stepped into the witness box and turned towards me. He was wearing his uniform but it was baggier on him than I remembered. He had grown a moustache since the last time I had seen him, and it made him look older. He smiled as if to reassure me that everything would be all right, and I smiled back. But I was afraid the situation was beyond his control. After a while I became aware of other eyes trying to intercept our gaze, to translate it for themselves, and so I looked away.

First of all my lawyer asked Morris how long we had been seeing each other. Morris mentioned a date. In an apologetic voice my lawyer then inquired what sort of relationship we had. Morris looked puzzled and said he wasn't sure what he was getting at. My lawyer asked if he had any intention of marrying me and Morris immediately stood up straight and in a very correct voice said, 'Yes, Your Honour. That is my intention.'

In answer to another question he named the regiment to which he belonged and where he was currently stationed. After a pause my lawyer commented that he obviously felt a strong sense of duty to King and Country, to which Morris replied, 'Yes. And my fiancée too.' But the lawyer seemed to find this answer confusing. He asked, 'Do you mean that your fiancée feels a duty to King and Country, or that you feel a duty to your fiancée?' Now it was Morris's turn to be confused. He looked at the judge and then at me, and then he smiled and said, 'Both.'

He was asked if I could be described as secretive. He thought about it and said, 'No, but not a blabbermouth either.' My lawyer wanted him to comment on the charges against me. Turning to the judge he announced that it was impossible. I was an honest person and besides, I was always too busy thinking about my patients. At that point the prosecutor asked how he explained the fact that I had posted anti-war stickers all over a certain neighbourhood. Morris looked at him coldly and said, 'It was a mistake. Everyone makes mistakes.' In a sardonic tone the prosecutor commented that some mistakes were more costly than others, and then announced that he had nothing more to say.

Just before he left the witness box Morris turned to me with that same confident smile. Looking at him I realised that he was nothing more than a prop, and it all came down to the lawyers, and which of them was the better actor. So from then on I watched them very closely, hardly noticing who passed through the witness box, until later in the afternoon, when my turn came to take the stand.

The witness box faced the jury and from the moment I entered it I realised that I would be standing directly in the old man's line of vision. There was a greasy stain on his tie and a crumb of toast in the corner of his mouth. The skin of his throat was raw and red as a dog's genitals, and punctured by stiff white bristles. The sight of him disgusted me, and yet I couldn't take my eyes off him. It was as if he was the only occupant of the jury box, as if he alone would be deciding my guilt or innocence. Every now and then he cupped a hand to his ear, and despite myself I raised my voice.

My lawyer asked me to describe the day I met Anna and I did, according to his earlier instructions, as briefly as possible. When I mentioned that I had bandaged a wound in her head he went off at a tangent and started to ask me in detail about my work. I couldn't see what bearing it had but I was happy to answer his questions because by then I knew it wasn't the truth that mattered, but how he presented it. So when he enquired why I had become a doctor in the first place, adding that it was an unusual career for a woman, I explained that the work had suited me, and I had found it interesting.

He wanted to know why I had come to the city, and why especially that neighbourhood, which was not, after all, the most desirable place to live. I replied that there was plenty of work for a doctor in that part of the city, and I had always been happy living there. I liked my flat and on the whole the people were friendly. The two women in the back of the jury box started whispering again but the old man just kept looking at me steadily. After a pause my lawyer half turned his back on me and asked if I regarded the preservation of human life important. The question struck me as absurd, and I said, 'What could be more important?'

The judge then asked me if I was a regular churchgoer – I said no – and if I believed in God. By this time I had abandoned all hope of finding a point to their questions and I replied that I had no reason to believe in him, but equally, no reason not to. I was reserving judgement. The judge scribbled something down and as I watched him I caught a slight movement out of the corner of my eye. Turning back to the old man I thought perhaps he had nodded. The expression on his face had changed, but only fractionally, and not enough to indicate what he was thinking. Perhaps it was a nod of approval. Then again, perhaps not. For the second time I realised there were things going on in this courtroom that had nothing to do with me.

The prosecutor's first question to me was, 'Do you consider yourself patriotic?' When I didn't answer immediately he rephrased the question and asked if I loved my country. It occurred to me that love wasn't what one felt for a country, but he was looking at me expectantly and so I replied, 'I was born here, and I choose to live here.'

'So you regard your nationality as an accident of birth?' he said, ironically. I was about to ask him what else it could be, if not an accident of birth, but he had already changed the subject, and started questioning me about Anna. They were questions I had answered a hundred times, and I replied as I had done a hundred times before. Some time later the court was adjourned and Crawford congratulated me on my performance. What the jury had seen this morning, he said, was a pillar of society with a strong sense of decency. The fact that I was a doctor would certainly work in my favour, he added, and at the very worst they would think that I had been led astray. I was surprised at this, but I didn't say anything.

When the court reconvened the defence called Benjamin Rose. He smiled and gave me a little wave, and I smiled back. I could tell he was nervous because he was twisting the felt rim of his hat in his hands. Each time he answered a question from one of the lawyers he called him 'Sir', and when my lawyer asked him to describe how I had helped his brother tears came into his eyes and he said, 'She saved his life, sir.' My lawyer then asked him to confirm that his brother had 'passed over', and Benjamin said, 'Two years ago. Cyril was in a lot of pain but because of her he died with dignity.' He was then asked what kind of a person I was and without hesitation he replied, 'A true Christian.'

In answer to another question Benjamin said that local people had been wary of a female doctor at first, and my lawyer interjected, 'That's understandable.' But Benjamin shook his head, saying, 'No.' According to him, I had been judged unfairly. But that was all in the past and I had earned their respect. My lawyer wanted to know if he had ever discussed politics with me and he replied that he couldn't remember ever having done so. But that wasn't surprising: anyone who knew him knew not to get him on the subject of politicians.

A couple of people laughed and Benjamin smiled and stood up a little straighter. He was enjoying himself now. But my lawyer thanked him and asked him to step down. He looked disappointed, but just before leaving he turned to me and nodded.

After Benjamin came the man who owned the café in the main road. He testified that I was a good customer and highly thought of in the neighbourhood. And then, finally, came Paul Janowitz. His name was called but it seemed like a long time before he entered the stand. When he did, he stood well back from the rail, with his arms hanging stiffly by his sides. Every few seconds he glanced in my direction, and looking at him, I had the impression that he was the one on trial.

My lawyer explained that he wouldn't be asking about the unfortunate affair of the policeman's death. That matter had been resolved separately and he merely required that the witness answer the questions put to him. Paul nodded. He was then asked to describe the events leading up to the stabbing, and how I had behaved. But he couldn't remember. The last time he remembered seeing me was when I had called to him from across the square. Then everything went hazy. He remembered 'that woman' running towards him, and he remembered the noise that the frightened birds had made. 'But then I was bleeding and all I could think of was the pain, and the knife lying at my feet.'

In a sympathetic voice the lawyer said it must be very distressing for him to have to relive the events. But Paul interrupted, saying there was one thing he remembered. He looked at me with something like relief and said: 'The woman was running towards me, and the doctor put out a hand to stop her.' He was then asked to describe me as a person. He replied that I was kind, and that I had always treated his sick mother with respect. He had heard that I had been responsible for posting the 'blackshirt' stickers but he found it hard to believe. Even if it was true, it didn't change the fact that I was basically a good person.

After Paul there were no more witnesses and it only remained for the lawyers to make their closing speeches. I was curious to hear what they had to say but I couldn't help feeling that nothing could sway the jury now. Their minds had been made up long ago. When the prosecutor came to sum up he reminded the jury of the expression 'no smoke without fire'. He asked them if it wasn't remarkable that whenever there was trouble I cropped up. First there was the incident with the policeman who died in the riot, then the stickers, then the radio station and finally the stabbing. He said, 'To argue that this is coincidence beggars belief.'

On the grounds that I had been associated with both a communist and a blackshirt, he went on, the defence would argue that I was not politically motivated. But that was plainly untrue. 'The woman you see standing before you, ladies and gentlemen of the jury, is an anarchist. You ask what motivates her. I will tell you. It is the end of law and order. The overturning of the establishment to make way for our enemies who, at this very moment, threaten the lives of our children!'

By this time the prosecutor's face was bright red and he was stabbing a finger in the air to emphasise his words. But suddenly he fell silent and collapsed into his chair, breathing hard. Slowly my lawyer got to his feet. He started by reminding the jury that nobody disputed the fact that I had posted subversive literature in public places. That might be sufficient grounds for detention, he said, but it was not a criminal offence. This was a complex case but it was the jury's duty to concentrate on the main issue: namely, whether or not I had collaborated with, or even instigated, the broadcasting of sensitive information to the enemy; whether I had been involved in any way with an illegal radio station; whether, indeed, I had acted treacherously. That was what they were being asked to decide, and nothing more.

All the time he spoke the old man watched me with his inscrutable expression, and the clock ticked on the wall. When the judge came to sum up, he impressed on the jurors the gravity of their task. At one point he said, 'It is difficult to imagine a more serious offence,' and I was reminded of the women on the remand wing who had jostled me in the corridors. The jury was then dismissed, and I was taken back down to the cells.

The jury was out for a long time. At least it felt like a long time, because there was no window or clock in the cell and I had no way of telling. I could have asked the wardress, of course, but I didn't like to break the silence, so I just sat and stared at the Sword of Justice on the wall in front of me.

Occasionally the wardress shifted in her seat. Each time it happened I glanced sideways at her, and the same thought went through my head: that we were in the same boat, and there was no difference between us. Finally I heard the jangling of keys and a policeman opened the door. As I passed him in the doorway he gave me a friendly smile and said, 'Good luck.' I was surprised and thanked him. When I reached the dock I deliberately avoided the old man's eyes, concentrating instead on the foreman: a fat man with glasses. Without prevarication the clerk asked what decision the jury had come to. Separating his words clearly, the foreman said, 'Not guilty.'

Then everyone seemed to talk at once, and beneath me Crawford actually clapped his hands and laughed out loud. Somebody patted me on the shoulder, but I don't remember who. Looking towards the old man I saw that his expression was the same and I thought at last I understood him. Either way, it's down to chance. That's what he was saying and it was true, even though justice had been done.

Crawford accompanied me out into the corridor. He talked incessantly but I didn't really pay attention, because the reality was sinking in: I didn't have to go back to prison. I was happy and at the same time fearful, because how was I to get home, with no money? And what would I do when I got there? I looked around, hoping to catch sight of Morris. It was then that I realised that this part of the courthouse, which I hadn't seen before, was very beautiful. Marble statues on pedestals lined the hallway. Higher up, painted figures danced across the vaulted ceiling, and separating the two was a long inscription. There wasn't time to read it all but I caught the words, 'Justice Equal Scales'.

We came to the top of a marble staircase and by now a little crowd of people had gathered behind us. I thought they must have mistaken me for someone else, because the public had been barred from my trial, and they couldn't possibly know the outcome. They were pushing and babbling excitedly and Crawford put his arm around my shoulders to protect me. Just then a man stepped out from behind a pillar at the foot of the staircase. He was wearing a macintosh, belted at the waist, and he had a thin, dark moustache. I think he was bewildered by all those people because he blushed and said, 'I'm sorry...'

We continued down the steps and the man climbed a few so that he was blocking our path. Crawford asked what he wanted and again he said, 'I'm sorry.' Impatiently Crawford put out a hand to push him aside but the man fended him off with his elbow. Then Crawford said, 'What is the meaning of this?' The stranger turned to me with a wild look in his eyes, and blurted out that he had orders to arrest me. The order for my detention had been renewed and I was to be taken straight back to the prison.

For a moment the babbling stopped and silence pressed on my eardrums. Then there was the sound of angry voices and shoe soles shuffling and screeching on marble. Someone grabbed my arm and pulled me away. Suddenly I was facing the crowd and the man in the macintosh was sitting, or rather sprawling, on the floor between us. He was dabbing at his nose and gazing in surprise at his bloodied fingers. Beyond him Crawford had raised his arms to keep the crowd back, and his horrified expression was mirrored in their faces. They had all turned to look at the place a few feet away where another man struggled in the grip of two policemen. It was Morris. His fists were clenched and he was shouting, but his words made no sense.

Finally, he seemed to realise it was hopeless. The policemen still held him by his arms but he sank to the ground, raising a hand to cover his eyes. I hurried across to him and whispered in his ear. I told him that he had done all he could, and the important thing was that I had been proved innocent. At the same time I knew it wasn't important at all, and yet there was nothing else I could say. The man in the macintosh was on his feet now, and I turned and nodded to him, to let him know I was ready to go.

Chapter 14

When I was first detained the way I accounted for it was that I had unwittingly broken the law. But when I was sent back for a second time, how could I explain it? A jury had found me innocent.

From then on, my biggest problem was thinking about the future. I wrote to Morris, asking him not to come any more, because each visit was a reminder of the passage of time. And I tried to lose track of the days. Days are just parcels of time, after all, and if I divided it up that way I'd always be wondering how many lay ahead. So instead of day and night, I began to think in terms of sleep and not sleep.

At first I kept to my normal routine, settling down after lights out and waking when the first rays of sunlight entered my cell. But as the months went by I found myself napping through the day. The more I slept, the more sleep I needed. My head was saturated and swollen with it. My waking thoughts became slower and more disjointed, while my dreams were more vividly real than I had ever known them. It was as if I had swapped one reality for another, or the two had somehow merged, and the upshot of it was that I couldn't always tell them apart. In my dreams I was always free. In that way, I was tunnelling out of there. But then something happened to remind me that it was all an illusion.

I was standing in the middle of my cell one night, undressing in the darkness, when the sirens started up. A moment later there was a great shuddering explosion nearby. A bomb had hit the perimeter wall. Afterwards I found out that it had crashed through the mains too. It shook the clay around the foundations and travelled in a shock wave through the floor of my cell. The wave continued up through my shin bones to my knees, so that I felt as if I were a part of the prison, and I had been hit too.

I looked up at the window. Yellow, crimson and orange flames flickered in the frosted glass. Watching them, it occurred to me that the bomb might have fallen through the roof of my cell. It might have killed me. And yet the prospect of death didn't frighten me. I knew then that to die suddenly would be better than this creeping suffocation. For the first time I understood why a woman would walk into the sea, or a man would want his sick brother dead. It was absurd to think that you could change your life. But you could end it.

Outside a siren grew louder, then stopped, and I knew that a fire crew had arrived to tackle the blaze. Some of their shouts filtered through the wall. I heard a man shout, 'Stem the flow!' and I was confused, because the flames still shimmered in the glass. But then an image flashed across my mind, of the prison rocking on a stormy sea, and firemen running to and fro, trying in vain to patch a hole in the hull. The water streamed through it, and for some reason my fellow prisoners and I were trapped on the outside. As the ship sank beneath the waves, we broke our fingernails clawing our way up to the higher portholes, trying to get in.

The door to my cell had been left open – it was prison policy during air raids – and the sound of sobbing reached me. It was coming from one of the other cells on the landing, and I had a sudden desire to shut it out. So I took hold of the heavy steel door and hurled it against the opening. Then I lay down on the bed, closed my eyes, and pressed my hands over my ears.

In the morning, a wardress found me huddled under my blanket, half dressed and facing the wall. Ever since they put the fire out in the early hours, I had felt an icy chill. I couldn't speak, or stop my teeth from chattering, and when she spoke to me, grabbing my shoulder and shaking it roughly, I couldn't understand what she was saying. I was glad when she finally left me alone. Slowly I rolled onto my back and opened my eyes.

By now I could reel off a precise inventory of the flaws in the walls and furnishings of my cell. So I was surprised to see two cobwebs growing down from the white-washed ceiling. I hadn't noticed them before. They resembled long streamers and what fascinated me most was that they drifted this way and that, in parallel, like tentacles of seaweed rooted to the ocean floor. I gazed up at them, and as I did so the air in my cell seemed to undergo a physical change. It grew glutinous and soupy, so that the cobwebs appeared magnified and the window shrunken, then undulated so that the cobwebs receded while the bars of the window rushed up close, and so on, back and forth.

I had the sense that I was looking through a prism, or a room-sized aquarium, and when I tried to move my legs

I couldn't. They were pinned to the mattress by a leaden cube of water that filled my cell. The edges of the cube were rigid but inside it the transparent fluid slid past itself in waves. It muffled my senses, blocking out the sounds of the prison, and when I tried to breathe the weight pressing down on my lungs prevented me. That was when I began to feel frightened. I had to take tiny sips of air and it was all I could do to raise my diaphragm for that.

Gradually I became aware that I was not alone. A number of people had entered the cell and their faces pulsated above me, looming in and out, distorted by the motion of the water. One was all in grey, and I recognised a wardress. The other (there were only two, after all) had on some long, white garment. I wanted to call out to them, but the weight on my chest was growing heavier by the second and I thought my ribcage would collapse.

Suddenly the cell disappeared from my vision and all I could see was a white expanse. Some clammy, eel-like creature moulded itself to my forehead and dragged back my eyelids, exposing the tops of my eyeballs to a cold draught. A deep booming filled my ears, and it occurred to me that my body had taken on the weight of a corpse. It was as if all my arteries had been squeezed shut and the blood prevented from circulating. I was certain I was dying, if not dead, and from that moment on fear left me. I was filled instead with a delicious knowledge of peace, because soon it would all be over and I would be free. I abandoned myself to that feeling, and in doing so, passed out.

When I woke I was no longer in my cell. I was lying

on a thin mattress with my cheek pressed against a wall. My first impression, again, was of dazzling white, and the soft texture of the wall. The weight had lifted from my body but now I was aware of a great pressure inside my head. I twisted my neck to see where I was. The room was of similar dimensions to my cell, except there was no window. There was no furniture, either, apart from the bed on which I lay and a stool in the corner. Sitting on the stool was a middle-aged woman in a white coat. Her iron-grey hair was tightly permed and there was a deep furrow between her eyes. She sat with her hands folded neatly in her lap, but when she saw that I was awake she got up and came towards me, peering down at me as if I was a dangerous animal.

I went to sleep again. I couldn't help it, the pressure in my head was too great. When I woke for the second time it had lessened a little, but I didn't have the energy to move. The woman had gone and I was alone. It was impossible to tell how much time had elapsed or whether it was night or day. The door, which was also padded and white, was closed, and there was no handle to it.

I lay very still, waiting for something to happen. Another woman entered, also wearing a white coat. She had long fingernails, painted red, and her lip curled in a disdainful way. She was carrying something in her hand: a white enamel kidney dish with a hypodermic needle in it. She placed it on the stool, then removed the syringe and, turning to face me, held it up to the light. It contained some colourless fluid. She flicked it with her nail and compressed the plunger so that a little fountain of liquid spurted out and splattered on the floor. I knew that it was a drug to dull my senses, but I didn't care. It made no difference to me if I was awake or asleep, alive or dead.

The doctor took hold of my arm and pushed my sleeve up roughly. I felt the point of the needle pierce my skin. Once the syringe was empty she removed it and placed it back in the dish. She stood looking down at me, holding the tray in her right hand, then turned and left the room.

A fog descended very slowly over my brain – I could almost see it – but I had time for one last thought. It occurred to me that I had come as far as I could along the path that I was on, and I was faced with a choice: either I stayed here, in this place with the white walls, or I turned round and set off back to where I had come from.

The next thing I remember is the doctor returning. She told me that I had been in that place for a day and a night. She asked me my name and that of the prime minister, and although I hesitated on the latter she seemed satisfied with my answers. She said, 'You've made a complete recovery,' and told me I was fit enough to return to my cell. But I couldn't remember being ill. All that had happened was that I had come to a realisation of how things were, and the shock of it had taken my breath away.

Chapter 15

The wardresses said I'd suffered a nerve storm. But I thought of it as a kind of enlightenment. Either way, it didn't matter, because from then on I began to look at things differently.

For instance, before I was sent to the prison hospital I had certain fixed ideas about freedom. Just the mention of the word would conjure up a set of images in my mind: a man sitting on the bow of a barge, waving like a king, a crowd cheering at a boxing match, Morris and I making love in an empty warehouse. To me, freedom meant all the things that I remembered most fondly about my former life. And each time my mind strayed towards them my heart would twist painfully, because I would be reminded of my loss.

Afterwards, though, I was able to contemplate freedom without that physical reaction. I'd think about it in a detached way, from a distance. It wasn't that I'd stopped hoping to be released. On the contrary, I wished for nothing more than to be able to sit on the end of my jetty again, with the sun warming my face, and my head resting on Morris's shoulder. But I'd realised that that kind of freedom, the freedom that is enjoyed outside prison, is an illusion. Because at any given moment a million people are conspiring to change the course of your life, not maliciously, but merely by exercising a freedom of their own.

As an example, I'd consider the time that Benjamin Rose came to see me at the surgery. It was then that he'd asked me to end his brother's life. But Cyril lived happily for months afterwards and died a natural death. If I'd done as Benjamin had asked, in the eyes of the world I would have been seen as a murderer. And rightly so: I would have deprived a man of life and happiness. But if Cyril had spent his last days writhing in agony, and I had refused to help him, then the world would have viewed me as innocent, and only Benjamin would have known my guilt. It was purely by accident, and a certain indecisiveness on my part, that I managed to avoid being a murderer at all.

By the same token, it was purely by accident that I had become a traitor. Just because one day, out of curiosity, I chose to walk back from my evening round via the main road rather than by the back streets, and a woman named Anna Petrova crossed my path. Just because it was wartime, and my neighbour was a communist. And just because of a host of other small details that I, unwittingly, had brought about. Circumstances converged to make a traitor out of me. And yet I didn't feel bitter, as I had in the past, because now I knew that what I had been deprived of was not my freedom, but the illusion of it.

It was only when I realised this that I managed, at last, to lose track of the days. You could say that I became oblivious to my surroundings. So that when the summons came for me to appear before the committee, I hardly noticed the journey to the hotel. I kept my eyes on the ground, and moved my feet in time with the pair in front.

It didn't strike me as strange that six of us women were being taken there at the same time, or that there were only two wardresses accompanying us. Nor did it strike me as strange that the hotel was crowded, with women lining the corridors and squatting on the steps, waiting to be seen; or that we marched straight past them and into the ballroom without a delay.

It was only when we had come to a halt, forming a row in front of the committee, that I raised my head and looked around me. The first things I noticed were the piles and piles of dossiers stacked precariously on the table, so that the chairman was almost completely partitioned off from his colleagues and had to lean back in his chair in order to confer with them. Files were stacked beneath the windows too, and up against the walls, almost reaching the height of the mirrors.

In one corner of the room, to the left of the table, Miss Miller was talking to a woman in a white coat. The woman had her back to me, but when she put up a hand to push back her hair, I saw that her long fingernails were painted red. At first I was surprised: I couldn't understand what the prison doctor was doing there. But then I looked at the faces of the women on either side of me, and it began to make sense. Each one had spent time in the hospital. All five had suffered nerve storms.

I was curious to see what bearing this would have on the proceedings. But the chairman was absorbed in his paperwork. He hardly seemed to know we were there. It was only when Miss Miller left the doctor and walked over to whisper something in his ear that he looked up with a startled expression and said, 'Ah, good!', as if he were the host, and we his long-awaited guests. Fumbling to adjust the pince-nez on his nose, he cleared his throat and began to speak.

To begin with I couldn't grasp what he was saying. There was a lot of legal jargon and he seemed to be mumbling into his shirt front. But I caught the phrase 'expert medical opinion'. Then he drew himself up and almost shouted the words, 'By the power vested in me... ' For the second time I had the impression that his was the voice of death, only on this occasion it held no fear for me. The black oval of his mouth flapped open and shut and something about it struck me as ridiculous, with the words gushing out of it, and the round pink face bursting out of the stiff white collar.

The chairman stopped talking and there was silence in the room. He was looking straight at me with an odd expression, and when I turned my head I saw that the other women were staring at me too. Then I realised: I was laughing out loud. I had thought it was just in my head. But I couldn't help it. My laughter rang round the room and echoed off the chandeliers. The next thing I knew, someone was pulling on my sleeve. I turned to see Miss Miller looking at me anxiously. She said, 'It's true, what he says. You're free. Understand? Free to go.'

I don't remember walking back through the hotel. But once outside I paid attention to my surroundings. I noticed, for instance, that it was summer, and that the country was still at war. The barrage balloons hung in the sky and the people in the streets were all dressed in drab colours: greys and browns and greens. But when we turned into the prison courtyard, I was confronted by a blaze of colour. The triangular flowerbeds were in bloom, and the sight of them filled me with secret hope.

We had to spend one last night in gaol. I was filled with a kind of excitement, but also doubt, because what if it wasn't true? What if I had dreamt it? Three years and four months I had spent in prison, but what if that was nothing compared to the years that stretched ahead? My head spun and I couldn't sleep. Instead I sat, fully dressed, on the edge of my bed, and watched the place on the floor where the bars waxed and waned with the moon.

In the morning, so as not to upset the other women, our cell doors were unlocked before the general reveille, and we were led out in silence. We walked along the landing, down the spiral staircase, across the centre, and through the maze of corridors that for so long had separated us from the world. There was a short delay in reception while we collected the belongings that had been taken from us, and signed a form, and then we were standing in glorious sunshine with the prison gates open in front of us.

At first nobody moved. But I saw the other women throw nervous glances at the street. I kept expecting a wardress to appear and order us back inside. It was impossible to believe that we were free; that all we had to do to rejoin our lives was to walk a few paces across a courtyard.

We stood there, uncertainly, until a man turned in at the gate. He wore a trilby hat and walked with a limp, and he was clutching a bunch of roses. His face immediately broke into a smile and he shouted a name. One of the women laughed in an embarrassed way and walked slowly towards him, glancing back at us over her shoulder. A moment later, a middle-aged woman wearing a mink stole and high heels appeared. She wasn't carrying flowers but her face split into a smile identical to the man's, and she quickened her step.

Next came Morris. He turned the corner quickly, his hands thrust deep into the pockets of his khaki trousers. When he saw me he stopped short, and his mouth fell open. But whether it was because of my appearance or just because I was there, in the open air, I couldn't say. His hair was blonder than I remembered it, and his face tanned. For the first time I noticed how like a boy's it was. And yet he had been my lover. The thought of it made me blush.

He stood where he was, staring at me, and his eyes filled with tears. I was surprised to see those tears, and at the same time a little disgusted. I couldn't shake the idea that I was looking at a stranger. He threw his arms around me and we stood there, in the courtyard, locked in an embrace. His skin gave off a faint smell of stale cigarettes. He held me like that for a long time and over his shoulder I looked out onto the empty street. All of a sudden that street looked very ordinary to me and I couldn't understand why I had yearned for it for so long.

Morris and I went to my flat. We caught the bus and walked the rest of the way. He didn't speak, and I was happy to keep the silence. But when we got there he took me by the hand and pulled me up the stairs, climbing them two at a time. Inside he took off his jacket and shirt. From the neck down he was the colour of cream. He smiled into my eyes and started to unbutton my blouse.

I didn't stop him: I was curious to see if a physical act would trigger my old feelings for him. But it didn't. I think that part of me had dried up or died. The only thing I remember about it was how soft the sheets felt beneath me.

Afterwards Morris lit a cigarette and talked. His eyes sparkled and he kept telling me how happy he was. He'd dreamed about this day. It was only the thought of it that had kept him going when he was fighting in Italy, crawling on his belly through the dirt and the undergrowth. All the men were the same: they knew they might die at any moment, so they had to keep making plans. For a soldier, it was the only way.

'We'll get married,' he said. 'I'll get my old job back at the factory and we'll start a family. A boy and a girl. But a boy first. How about it?' I didn't say anything and he laughed. 'All right,' he said, 'A girl first.' But still I didn't reply. I was thinking about what he'd said, and how in prison I'd tried so hard to forget about the future. It didn't matter, though, and there was no harm in making plans, as long as you didn't allow yourself to be disappointed.

I got up and Morris watched me dress. I told him I wanted to go for a walk. He said, 'I'll come too,' but I said, 'No.' I wanted to go alone. His face fell and he looked a little hurt. But then he smiled and said he'd wait for me.

It was ten o'clock in the morning. No sound came from the Janowitzes' flat. But for all I knew the old lady had died, or they had moved away. Perhaps Paul was a soldier now. Out in the street people were milling about, going about their daily business, but no one paid any particular attention to me. I was no longer an object of curiosity. And yet I studied the face of each person who passed me. I couldn't help feeling that just by being there, so close to them, I was in some kind of danger. At any moment, any one of them might say something, or do something, to upset the delicate balance of my life. A complete stranger might change it forever. A part of me felt sad, because never again would I feel free. I'd always be plagued by this sense of helplessness. But another part of me was curious to know how it would happen, and who would be responsible.

I turned into a street with factories on one side and houses on the other. A bomb had fallen in the night, destroying one house and half of the next. All that was left was a great mound of rubble and a single chimney. I'd seen it all before, on my outings to the hotel, and yet it shocked me. Thick hosepipes lay along the gutter and the cobbles were awash with water. A red fire engine was parked across the street and beside it an ambulance. Men in uniform scrambled up and down ladders, scaling the mountain of debris and hacking at it with picks and shovels.

A little crowd had gathered on the opposite pavement and as I came up to it a woman groaned and clapped her hand over her mouth. Another, younger, woman uttered a cry and started sobbing. I turned towards the ruin and saw a man on a stretcher. He was strapped to it and two ambulance men were negotiating a ladder and trying to juggle the stretcher between them at the same time. At one point it looked as if the patient was standing on the shoulders of the man beneath. But he was unconscious, slumped against the canvas. His head was misshapen and one of his ears was missing. His face and clothes were soaked with blood and dirt.

I stopped to watch and one of the women told me what had happened. She spoke in a thick voice, as if holding back tears. The man on the stretcher was the husband, she told me. The wife had come out first, but they hadn't been able to save her. The boy was still inside. A fireman had called down to him, and he'd answered. His leg was trapped, and he was bleeding. So they were digging as fast as they could to get him out. But the whole house had fallen in on top of him. And he was getting weaker by the minute. 'It's not right,' she said, shaking her head.

I walked on. I was sorry about the boy but there was nothing I could do and I didn't want to get involved. A man wearing a straw hat stopped to ask me directions to the nearest police station. When I didn't speak he frowned, touched the rim of his hat, and hurried on. It was only then that I realised my mistake. He had genuinely wanted to know the way. But I had been waiting for him to tell me that there had been some misunderstanding; that he had another order for my arrest. It was that same feeling of helplessness and I couldn't free myself of it.

When I reached the river I turned west and walked along the embankment. I walked for several hours, not thinking about where I was going, but just enjoying the sunshine and the fact that I could take any turning I liked. When repair works blocked my path I turned north, winding through the side streets until I found myself at Anna's restaurant. I was surprised to see it, but then I realised that this was where I had been heading all along. The gold paint was flaking off the letters and the windows had been boarded up. But where one of the planks had slipped the glass behind was visible. Someone had thrown a brick and shattered it. On the door a sign that read 'Under New Management' hung from a single nail. It had been defaced.

I was standing there, taking it all in, when I noticed a small boy at my elbow. He might have been standing there for some time. He held out his hand and told me that he knew a way in. For sixpence he'd show me the 'famous spy's' bedroom. I ignored him and turned away. But a few minutes later, when I stopped to listen to an organ grinder, and his assistant came up to me with a beseeching look, holding out his cap, I found that my pocket was empty. The money that Morris had given me for a bus fare had gone. Now I would have to walk home. It didn't matter though and I was happy to do so. I couldn't imagine ever feeling tired, and the idea suddenly came to me of going to my place by the river. The jetty was gone, but I could still climb down onto the shore and find a place to sit quietly.

I retraced my steps and when I reached the street where the house had been bombed, I found it deserted. The fire engine and the ambulance had gone and the crowd had dispersed. It was three in the afternoon. The air shimmered with the heat and the cobbles burned the soles of my feet. There was a smell of scorched wood and on the opposite side of the road the rubble still smouldered. A yellow dog was running up and down the edge of it, sniffing. But it kept returning to one particular spot and yapping loudly.

I crossed the road, not out of curiosity, but under a sort of inertia. I didn't want to, I'd much rather have kept going and reached the jetty before the day cooled, but I couldn't stop myself. Something drove me on. When I got there, I thought I heard a noise. It sounded like wood creaking, or a muffled cry. But the dog was yapping and I couldn't be sure. I shooed it away and listened. Nothing came, though, and I thought I must have imagined it. I felt a huge wave of relief, because now I could carry on my way. But just as I was turning to go I heard it again: a child's voice. It was no more than a murmur, and yet it must have been close to the surface. Perhaps he had crawled into a space. But he couldn't have: his leg was trapped. The woman had told me so.

Reluctantly, and with that same feeling of inevitability, I placed my hand on a brick and pulled it away. There was a little cascade of dust. The dog yapped once, took a few paces towards me and, lifting a paw off the ground, cocked its head on one side. I looked around. The factories on the other side of the road were shut up and silent. Nobody had seen me. But the dog fixed me with its beady eyes and it was as if it was demanding something of me. Then the sound came again. I pulled another brick out, and then another, until I was able to remove a large plank of wood. There was another cascade but this time the debris fell inwards and I heard a child's cough, very weak.

I peered into the hole. It was pitch black inside, and I couldn't see. Dust filled my nostrils and I turned away to sneeze. But when I pushed my head back in two brilliant discs of light shone up at me: the child's eyes. He was only a few yards away, but lower, beneath the level of the road. A second later the eyes vanished and there was nothing but darkness and silence. It occurred to me that he had drifted into unconsciousness, that he was near death. If I got down on my knees I could dig down to him. I might be able to save him. And yet I didn't move.

Why not, I couldn't say. But looking back on it, I think it was at that moment that something snapped inside me. All of a sudden I was filled with a terrible rage. What right had this boy to expect me to save him? But in fact my rage wasn't directed against him, but against the circumstances in which he and I found ourselves. Why had the bomb fallen here, rather than on the empty factory opposite? Why couldn't I be allowed to keep walking and reach the jetty before the warmth went out of the sun? And if I did help him, why would that be a good thing? What if he grew up to be a murderer, or a spy? That deed might make me a good person now, but in hindsight I would be judged differently. Then the world might be glad I had kept walking. The passage of time would vindicate me. Because nothing in this world was good or bad. Nothing was certain, nothing at all. It made no difference if I helped the boy or not. Better just to leave him, better not to get involved.

The dog ran up to me and yapped again. But I kicked it away. And then I replaced the plank, and the two bricks, and turned and walked towards the river.

THE END

THE END

The main character of this book is loosely based on a woman who, during the Second World War, was detained in Holloway Prison, London under Regulation 18B of the Defence (General) Regulations. She was one of relatively few British citizens, compared to the tens of thousands of enemy aliens, who were rounded up in the spring of 1940 on suspicion of being involved in Fifth Column activities.

Detainees were held without trial, charge, or term set, but what made this woman's case unique was that after her initial detention, she was tried, acquitted, and detained again. Her name appeared on weekly lists of 'Prominent Persons' held under the regulation that Winston Churchill asked to receive during the early days of its use. Although not the architect of 18B, Churchill was a keen supporter of it. Later he came to regret his role in what he saw as a gross invasion of civil liberty.

ACHILLES

Elizabeth Cook

'An instant classic. I have never read anything like it'
Kate Kellaway, *Observer*

This powerful, passionate and beautifully crafted retelling of the
epic tale of Achilles recreates Homer's fated hero in a new and vivid
reality. Elizabeth Cook's mesmerising poetic voice weaves the
interlocking stories of Achilles and the central figures of his legend
into a many-layered exploration of achievement and loss, of
choice and inescapable destiny.

'Extraordinary, and extraordinarily successful . . . what the late
Angela Carter did for the folk-tale or fairy-story, Cook is here
doing for the classical epic'
Sara Maitland, *Spectator*

'A masterful retelling of the myth – a short, intense account
of a short, intense life, closer to being a poem than a novel:
if not verse, then at least prose with blood pressure'
Thomas Jones, *London Review of Books*

SELECTED FICTION TITLES AVAILABLE FROM METHUEN

ISBN	TITLE	AUTHOR	PRICE
☐ 0413 52890 1	Collected Short Stories	Bertolt Brecht	£9.99
☐ 0413 77139 3	Achilles	Elizabeth Cook	£6.99
☐ 0413 59970 1	Collected Short Stories	Nöel Coward	£12.99
☐ 0413 75360 3	Been Here and Gone: A Memoir of the Blues	David Dalton	£10.99
☐ 0413 77160 1	The Name of the World	Denis Johnson	£6.99
☐ 0413 75960 1	A Wild People	Hugh Leonard	£15.99
☐ 0413 74660 7	I Don't Need You Any More	Arthur Miller	£7.99
☐ 0413 74670 4	Plain Girl	Arthur Miller	£6.99
☐ 0413 74900 2	Between Us Girls	Joe Orton	£6.99
☐ 0413 41460 4	Head to Toe	Joe Orton	£6.99
☐ 0413 76290 4	Sweet Hearts	Melanie Rae Thon	£6.99
☐ 0413 75710 2	Revolutionary Road	Richard Yates	£6.99
☐ 0413 74700 X	Layover	Lisa Zeidner	£6.99

● All Methuen books are available through mail order or from your local bookshop, or online at www.methuen.co.uk.

Please send cheque/eurocheque/postal order (sterling only) Access, Visa, Mastercard, Diners Card, Switch or Amex.

☐☐☐☐☐☐☐☐☐☐☐☐☐☐☐☐

Expiry Date: _____ Signature: _____

UK customers please allow £1 for the first book and 50p thereafter up to a maximum of £3 for postage and packing.

Overseas customers please allow £1.50 for the first book and 75p thereafter up to a maximum of £5 for post and packing.

ALL ORDERS TO:

Methuen Books, Books by Post, TBS Limited, The Book Service, Colchester Road, Frating Green, Colchester, Essex CO7 7DW.

NAME: _____

ADDRESS: _____

_____

_____

Please allow 28 days for delivery. Please tick box if you do not wish to receive any additional information ☐

Prices and availability subject to change without notice.